WLA Folios: Home

Copyright © 2019 War, Literature & the Arts
All rights reserved.
ISBN-13: 9780578497396

Cover: Quilt "Soldier On" by Lucy Sattler.
Design by William Newmiller

TABLE OF CONTENTS

Jesse Goolsby and Katie Witt – **Editors' Note** 1

Kate Gaskin – **Poem in Which You Leave** 2

Cristina Fríes – **Sister, Answer Me** 5

Philip Metres – **Dispatch from Russia in the Long Cold War** 8

Lynn Marie Houston – **My Father Sends Me a Card That Says You Are So Loved** 21

Sara Nović – **On Late-Stage Pediatric Cardiomyopathy** ...23

Lucy Sattler – **Artist's Statement** 33

Drew Pham – **Because of George H.W. Bush, I Thought Smart Bombs Were a Good Thing** 42

David Morris – **Pro Patria** 46

Marléne Zadig – **Soldier's Joy** 54

Kim Garcia – **Homelands** 67

M.C. Armstrong – **Wapakoneta** 69

Bix Gabriel – **Once** 86

JESSE GOOLSBY & KATIE WITT

EDITORS, *WLA FOLIOS*

For thirty years, *War, Literature & the Arts: An International Journal for the Humanities* has featured art across all genres as it pertains to humanity's engagement with the many different aspects of conflict and its aftermath.

This year's theme for *WLA Folios* is Home. Through fiction, poetry, essay, and texture, we are honored to share twelve talented voices with you here.

We hope you enjoy the issue and investigate *WLA*'s entire catalogue at wlajournal.com.

KATE GASKIN

Poem in Which You Leave

Springtime, the azaleas
in pink fire, the baby there

beside the rocking chair
on my parents' front porch.

And you are where?
Here is a monotony

of baby gear, the swing
that clicks him side to side,

a small origami
of laundry, loose bottles,

frozen rings for his teeth,
one breast that gives

and the other that gives
up its milk in grief.

*

He is rolling over
front to back, back to front

as you crouch
in the desert and cradle

your phone. A miracle
to see it at all

from so many miles, the planes
that drone, the wind

that scabs the brush, your face,
the crust of salt and dust

you wear like skin.
Again, you say. Again.

*

And tease me, my boots,
my kin, the wind

in my hair down Elkahatchee
Creek, the shed skin

of ribbon snakes the summer when
we chased Hale-Bopp

down our neighborhood streets.
I did not want to come home

to this, you gone, the ghost
of my legs whitening in the lake,

you kissing me,
you kissing me and then—

*

When you left
I dug our wretchedness

up like a bulb and moved it
back home while you flew

off to war. Now I nurse
from my right side

as the catalpa trees
flush white

and the yard weeds over
in bright green.

———

KATE GASKIN is the author of *Forever War* (YesYes Books 2020), which won the Pamet River Prize. Her poems have appeared or are forthcoming in *Guernica, Pleiades, The Southern Review,* and *Blackbird* among others. She is a recipient of a Tennessee Williams Scholarship in poetry to the Sewanee Writers' Conference, as well as the winner of *The Pinch*'s 2017 Literary Award in Poetry. She lives in Omaha, Nebraska.

CRISTINA FRÍES

Sister, Answer Me

Sister, you who are so tall and can see out the window when I cannot, tell me, is that the sound of our mother coming home? It is late, I am sleepy, and I want to be held in her arms.

No, it is not our mother, but a black truck swerving into our circular driveway, driving over the rose bushes, and parking on the front lawn.

Sister, you who are older than me, tell me, is that the sound of our neighbors knocking on the window to check that we are safe and warm on this night like many others when father has gone looking for our mother?

No, it is not our neighbors, but five men trying to open a downstairs window, and oh, rejoicing as they slide themselves like snakes into our home.

Sister, are you sure? Put your ear against the bedroom door and tell me, is that not the sound of our friends sneaking into the kitchen to make you a cake for your birthday tomorrow?

No, they are not our friends, but men opening the refrigerator, smashing the bottles of cider and shoveling handfuls of tonight's spaghetti into their mouths.

Sister, you whose stories always make me feel less afraid, tell me, is that the sound of our father coming to swear that he will never drive mother out of the house again?

No, be quiet, it is not our father, but someone filling duffel bags with laptops, jewelry, bottles of aged wine, knocking mother's vases onto the floor.

Sister, you who used to tell me to ignore anything unpleasant that happens outside our bedroom, tell me, can't we ignore these intruders?

No, we cannot ignore them, they are five desperate men who will do anything to feed their children.

Sister, you who invited the whole school to your seventeenth birthday tomorrow, open the door now and tell these men to leave us alone so that you can be celebrated by two hundred strangers, get drunk, sneak a boy up to your room again, which is what you want, isn't it, to distract mother and father from their fighting?

No, I won't let those men find us. Come and we will hide in the closet.

Sister, if our problems are ours and theirs are theirs, isn't it true that I can open the bedroom door and watch them pass through our home like ghosts that will never truly hurt us?

No, these men are real, and if you open the door, we will not go unseen and unheard as we are by our parents.

Sister, I've opened the door, and can see them stripping the paintings off the walls. They've heard you gasp, and now they see us in the shadow of the doorway. Tell me, why are they looking at us so fearfully?

They are surprised to see us, and now that they've entered our room, they have no choice but to push us onto the bed, and bind our wrists and ankles with zip ties, as they are now. See what you've done? They've covered our heads with those bags, and now we cannot see.

Sister, you who have recently grown so distant from me, walking around like you think you live not here but on the moon, tell me, aren't these men just an empty threat, and years from now when we are older and have married, become artists like we've always wanted, and rich ourselves, won't tonight's events only seem like a small blip in an otherwise beautiful and distant dream?

Sister, answer me. I heard the bed squeak once, and now the weight of you beside me is gone, but tell me, sister, are you still thinking of an answer to my question, which is so dependent on what happens next, that you cannot tell me yet, not yet, and still, not yet?

CRISTINA FRÍES is a fiction writer. Her story "New Years in La Calera," published originally in EPOCH Literary Magazine (Vol. 66 No. 3), won a PEN America Award. She is pursuing an M.A. in Creative Writing at UC Davis, and is at work on a collection of short stories.

PHILIP METRES

Dispatch from Russia in the Long Cold War

It seems as if every U.S. media story about Russia revolves around Russia's meddling in our democracy and helping us to elect an autocrat. I'm as fascinated as anyone by the sudden resurgence of a Cold War, with its stories of Russian spies living secret lives as Americans and the exploits of the dictatorial Vladimir Putin, whose shirtless and botoxed reign seems both bizarre and yet completely understandable, given Russian history. And yet, Russia—its enigmatic people, its cruelty and kindness, its troubled beauty and crazy lovely culture—slips from our self-interested and misunderstanding grasp.

Twenty-five years ago, I was drawn to that puzzle of a country—where it was said that poets recited their work to stadiums and were feared by the regime—to witness to the dramatic historical change after the Soviet Union fell, and to meet the poets who helped make it fall. I wanted to slip behind the formerly Iron Curtain, and the curtain of images that we associated with that place. To see it for myself. What I found was more surprising and more mundane than I could have imagined. Nearly four months into my stay, my family came to visit, which is the occasion for this story, a glimpse into a Russia that you couldn't read in the news then, and you won't read in the news now.

***

"How can he even see?" my father said, shaking his head at the taxi cab's damaged front windshield, as the driver scurried in the winter cold to fit the suitcases, Tetris-like, into the shallow trunk. Running from left to right, diagonally downward, a huge crack scarred the front glass, like a lightning bolt frozen in flight. It was December, 1992.

"Whoa," Dave, my twelve-year-old brother, said, elbowing my sister, Kath, toward the jalopy and its windowscreen.

They stuffed themselves into the tiny car like clowns in scarves and down coats—Mom and Kath and Dave in the back, Dad riding shotgun, next to their unnamed chauffer. Once inside, the view of Russia was no better. Everything outside was split into two, or more than two, if you counted the webbing of smaller cracks. You just had to get used to seeing through cracks.

A few minutes earlier, they'd drowsily stumbled through Moscow security and emerged onto the other side, into Russia, looking for me. I'd told them over the staticky phone line that I'd meet them at the airport, but I was nowhere to be found. I'd been living there for four months already, on a fellowship to study Russian poetry, and they'd come to visit this enigmatic land, this strange place that had sucked in their son.

They spotted a driver holding a brown cardboard sign: Metres.

"Where's Phil?" my mother asked the man, a sharp panic cutting through her dull sleepiness.

"No English," he said, shaking his head, and grabbing my mother's suitcase, gestured for them to follow. "Come."

My dad hesitated. Were they being kidnapped? The Cold War had ended, but how could they trust the Russians? This Russian? All he had was a sign with their name on it. Visions of the Lubyanka Prison swirled before him, the cornucopia of techniques that make people talk. But no one else appeared from the amoebic mass of unknown faces. They had no choice but to follow this anonymous man through the suddenly-parting crowd.

"Is *this* the country we feared?" my dad wondered aloud from the front seat, laughing in astonishment, looking out at the cobwebbed vision of Russia. He'd been stunned by the dingy airport. The smell of the public bathroom in the airport almost made him puke—not just the ammoniac scent of old piss, but the raging nastiness of decaying shit. The toilet looked like it hadn't been cleaned since Stalin died. And the only thing to wipe your ass with was little shreds of yellowed newspaper. He'd staggered out like a punch-drunk boxer, trying to keep his insides intact. And now, the creaky car and its thunderstruck windshield, the battered highway road, the driving without the headlights on in the pitch dark. How wrecked the country seemed.

Nothing about this place was what he'd imagined. Having spent his entire life under the shadow of the Cold War, his adult years serving in the Navy and Navy Reserve, he could hardly believe his eyes. Could this be the mighty Soviet Union? The fearsome order of marching troops and tanks and missiles parading across Red Square? The Duck and Cover drills in case of a nuclear attack, hiding beneath his desk in elementary school. A thought began to itch away in his brain. What if the whole thing was a grand fiction? Not just that the Soviet Union had bluffed about its strength, but that America had wanted them mightier, more sinister than they were.

He turned to Kath, his daughter, in the back seat.

"I remember when I was your age, I watched the news during the Cuban Missile Crisis in the dorm common room. I thought it was only a matter of time before I was called up."

"Were you scared?" she said.

"Everyone was scared. The world seemed so close to war," he said, casting his eyes over the hulking white apartments, massed at the edge of the city.

The intimidating military force, combined with godless communism, for which the ends justified the means, meant that we would have to stop at nothing to stop them. And yet, as he looked around, recalling the great fear, he couldn't understand why everything in Russia seemed so dilapidated. If they couldn't afford new windshields and headlights, if they couldn't give the buildings a new coat of paint, how could they have ever have won a war?

He couldn't keep looking, and his head hurt to think of what he'd seen, so he sat back in his seat, closed his eyes.

By the time they arrived at the apartment, the winter moon was bright, and they looked eagerly past Olya when she opened the door.

"Where's Phil?" my mother asked, her fatigue tilting toward confusion and worry.

"At hospital," Olya chirped in her rudimentary English, trying to explain my absence but not getting much farther than "hospital." They knew I'd been living there with Olya, a middle-aged physicist who not only rented me a room, but cared for me like an overgrown son. Still, they were alarmed by my absence. Olya fluttered about, trying to fit them into slippers and ply them with tea, trying to settle them into the two room apartment, which only increased my mother's panic, which in turn elevated Olya's fluttering, her tone now roughly somewhere between soprano and glass-breaking.

Earlier that day, I'd been burning in the oven of fevers, wrapped in blankets in the wreckage of my couch-bed, my face swollen almost twice its size and covered with undetermined spots. I was trying not to die of a mysterious illness that looked like measles but felt as if demons were attempting to drag me beneath the soil to the center of the earth. I could feel how hot it was already, and I was sweating through clothes every few hours, just to make sure that I'd either to freeze to death or burn in Hell.

It seemed a metaphor for my entire time in Russia. I'd arrived in humid early September, eager to delve into this country where poets were admired by the people and feared by tyrants, where suffering seemed noble, and everything felt real. I'd been repelled by the bloodlust of my own country in the wake of the bizarre media coverage of the Persian Gulf War, where it appeared that no one died and that smart bombs were heroes. The worst part was that my fellow citizens appeared to revel in the lie. I couldn't wait to see the truth of Russia, knowing that it too had been enveloped in a cloud of Cold War fictions and deception.

But by the thick of winter, in loneliness and despair, I'd seen Russia's own problems all too clearly, knew them in my bones, and now was wracked in the rack of delirium. I gave up my solo battle against the fever-demons and decided to take a cab to a clinic, to see if a doctor might figure out my complicated case.

When I opened the door an hour later, everyone rushed to the foyer and, after examining my face and smothering me in hugs, drowned me with questions. Yes, I was at the only American health center in Moscow. No, an indistinguishable disease. Yes, sometime around Christmas. Yes, after a week of sweating and delirium, I could no longer ignore it. Yes, that's why I wasn't at the airport to greet them. Yes, some medicine that would at least help me breathe and not discover the magic of spontaneous combustion.

"It's okay, Mom," I said, "I think I'm getting better." One side of my face looked better than the other, so I turned that side toward them, trying not to worry them. The country looked like shit, and I looked like shit, and seemed as if it and my face might collapse or explode at any moment. Ever since I'd arrived, I'd fallen into one hole or another—literal potholes in roads, of course, but also colds and fevers, water shortages and power outages, byzantine train schedules and overstuffed sweaty local buses, angry cashiers and overprotective hosts, urinating public drunks and desperate stares, communist protestors and capitalist prostituki, insomnia and depression, bitter cold and murderous cold, unnameable feelings and unpronounceable words—so many holes beneath my feet and around my head. But suddenly, with my parents and my sister and brother now here, I wondered, maybe—just maybe—I and the country would survive.

I'll have to trust my sister's memory on the Pizza Hut order, since I was still somewhere between delirious and demented. The background is this: that fall, not one, but two Pizza Huts had appeared suddenly in Moscow. The first Pizza Huts in Russia. I'd been amazed when a window—not a hut, but a mere window—had opened on Tverskaya Boulevard, offering personal pan pizzas. It was a window in one of the usual stone buildings, but there appeared to be no way to enter from the street. Still, a Pizza Hut window! It was the equivalent of finding out that your closet had a portal to a world called Narnia. A cheesy, butter-crusted Narnia.

It was one of the few windows in Russia you could approach to purchase something and not get castigated or turned away for some unknown reason.

I mostly avoided it, trying to do my best to live like a Russian.

"Pizza Hut" in Russian sounds more like "Pizza Hat," if the "h" were aspirated in a way that makes it sound like you were suffering from a sore throat, and probably need to expectorate.

My family was relieved that I wasn't going to die. But they were also hungry.

Pizza Hut, the new telephone directory suggested, was now offering delivery—a fact that seemed as fanciful as demons that drag people into Hell or letters that could travel through a phone line.

The possibility of pizza brought directly to the apartment was too delicious and warm to pass up. After all, it was approximately minus 72 degrees outside, also known as the number when Centigrade actually sounds better than Fahrenheit.

My father made the call, and asked for a cheese pizza.

"Margarita?" the Pizza Hut man replied.

"No, no, cheese pizza," my dad tried to explain, using louder tones, in case the line was staticky, or the way one speaks louder as if to express one's increasingly beset will and to make children do as they're told.

There was a click and the line went silent.

I told them to wait. If there was anything I'd learned since I'd come to Russia, is that you can wait much longer than you think you can.

"And by the way, 'margherita' just means cheese pizza," I said.

Fifteen minutes later, my dad said, "FUCK THIS," and hung up. He tried to call the other Pizza Hut location, but our phone was dead.

"Maybe," I suggested from inside the oven, "the neighbors were using the shared line."

So I limped over to the neighbors' door and inquired. They weren't using the phone.

After fifteen more minutes, the phone was working again. Apparently the K.G.B. was sufficiently pleased with our persistence and gave us an open line.

Dad asked for a "margherita."

"There is a fifty dollar minimum," the Pizza Hut man retorted.

"We only want one pizza," my dad said.

"You could order beer," his nemesis declared.

Dad deflected the attempts to sell us beer and took another tack. "How about a salad," my dad said, as if to negotiate a truce.

One hour later, the pizza arrived. Upon opening the box, we saw that the pizza was cold. Very cold. Ice crystals had formed on top.

Our oven, sadly, wasn't working. It was the gas line, no doubt, which occasionally decided to go on holiday. I offered to warm the pizza next to my feverish body.

The salad, the key to completing this accord between hostile powers, consisted of yellowed cabbage, dry onion, canned peas, and tomatoes from the 19th century.

We feasted like serfs.

A day later, in the biting cold, my friends Dima and Natasha took my family to visit Red Square, with me still wrapped in a half-dozen blankets, my face slowly returning to its former size. But my father was worried. He'd just retired from the military, and here he was on enemy territory, without any security, not even a knife or a sidearm. When they got off the Metro at Krasnaya Ploschad, he glanced in both directions, looking for suspicious men, wondering which of them would be the kidnappers.

There were fewer people on the street than the previous day, given the biting arctic wind, and everyone was bundled from head to foot, with great fur *shapkas* pulled tight around their heads, even the ear flaps pulled down and tied beneath their chins. They looked more like starving bears than KGB agents. My mom was freezing in her thin red cashmere overcoat, as I had been some months before, in my own cashmere coat, learning the same lesson about appropriate winter wear.

Still, a woman was selling ice cream, banging the lid of the gray metal cooler against the top with her mittened hands, trying to attract customers. *MoROzhenoye*! she cried into the cold, as if to keep herself warm. A couple walked away, licking vanilla cones in their mittened hands. He couldn't believe their tongues didn't just stick to the ice cream.

And then, before him: Red Square, where the Red Army marched and flexed its fearsome muscles, smaller than he'd imagined, perhaps the size of a couple football fields, from St. Basil's on the far end to where he stood now. On one side, the pale yellow Kremlin wall, and on the other, a shopping mall. Nestled near the Kremlin wall, the Lenin Mausoleum, where the old visionary murderer lay like a greasy pancake, ready for viewing, if not consuming.

A few years later, when he returned with some Navy comrades to Vietnam for the first time in forty years, they were stunned to see that the country they remembered—the country that simply meant "the war" so that you didn't have to say "the Vietnam War," just "Vietnam"—the country they'd carried with them in their skulls and bodies over the years, all the hurts and worries and griefs and smells and confusions and glories and memories, that country no longer existed. How strange it was, to walk around that burgeoning metropolis with the shiny skyscrapers and a new name—no longer Saigon but Ho Chi Minh City—and have almost nothing that recalled that time. And relief, relief that Vietnamese people had moved on, that they weren't murderous or even angry at Americans for what had happened.

In Moscow, at the heart of this stubborn country, my dad could not get over what he was seeing.

"Red Square," he said, not knowing what else to say, stopped on the cobbles, leaning over and placing his hands on his knees, standing inside the heart of enemy territory.

And the next day, when I was at least feeling human, we all took the train to Kaliningrad to meet the Maslovs, the family who'd taken care of me during my first months.

Along the way, a leak developed in the traincar, and began to drip directly onto my head, as if the whole universe had wanted me to stay in bed. Still, at the station, when we tumbled out of the car, Valera Maslov and his friend were there to greet us, and ushered us into their cars, to drive back to their three-room apartment. In the warm interior, behind Svetlana Maslov and her son Alyosha, Svetlana's father Nikolai stood, dignified and quiet. His beard was white and well-groomed, and he was gentle and frail with the years. The Maslovs had been so good to me, treating me like family, and now my two families greeted each other, each trying on the other's native tongue, before sitting at the table in what was Valera and Svetlana's bedroom, and also their living room, and now also their dining room. The feast before us was the usual and astonishing array of Russian classics—shredded beet vinaigrette, the Olivier potato salad, and, of course, caviar—astonishing because I knew how hard it was not only to prepare, but to find and buy.

"Delicious," my mother said.

"Delicious," I said in Russian.

"Thank you," my mother said.

"Thank you," I said in Russian. And we were off. Despite my aching brain, my Russian tongue did not fail me. I translated everything, and it was a wonder to everyone including myself—that after four months, I'd gone from a deaf-mute child to a bilingual adult, my feverish tongue a bridge between my parents' English shore and the Maslovs' Russian one.

When all the courses were done—the salads, the soup, the meat, and the dessert, and we'd all gone quiet with contentment, Nikolai stood up from the table.

He pulled something colorful and shiny from his pocket, and held them up.

"These are from the war, the Great Patriotic War," Nikolai said.

They were ribboned medals—golden-coined commemorative pieces that Nikolai had earned for his service to the Motherland.

The last war when Americans and Russians fought on the same side, to defeat fascism, their armies meeting in Germany, Hitler dead from a self-inflicted wound, in his fuhrerbunker.

Nikolai put his hand out to my father, who'd stood up when his fellow soldier had stood.

"There should be peace and friendship," he said, "between the people of great nations."

My father hesitated, not believing what he was seeing.

"Thank you," he said, putting his right hand over Nikolai's hand as he opened his left hand to receive the gift.

On New Year's Eve, Olya told me that she would be celebrating with some friends at their place, to give my family some space. The six of us including Olya had been packed into two rooms, sleeping on every available couch, and I thanked her again for opening her small apartment to my people.

"It's nothing," she said, and bid us farewell as we tromped back out into the tundra.

It was so quiet on the streets, and even in the Metro. No one spoke.

"Did you ever notice," my mom whispered, leaning in, "how quiet people are here? No chatter, no noise at all."

I shook my head. I had grown accustomed to their stoic silence.

"It's beautiful," she said. "Almost like prayer."

After a day exploring the city again—in which my little brother showed a remarkable code-breaking ability, navigating the Metro's daunting Cyrillic alphabet with my father to get to the Arbat to seal some deals for fur hats—we returned together to the apartment that evening tired, cold, and hungry. My mom went into the kitchen to put some tea on.

"Everyone, come in!" she called, almost immediately. "You won't believe it."

Two candles flickered on the table, casting a calming glow over the table, where a whole meal was laid out for us—borscht and pickled salad, cheese and bread. The tea water was still hot. Olya was nowhere to be found.

"That's so typical of her," I said. "Some kind of magic."

The Pizza Hut order was Russia, but this was also Russia, a Russia that kept surprising us, unfolding unanticipated layers alternating between bitter and sweet. Just when I thought I couldn't endure it any longer, its utter nonsensicality, its newspaper toilet wipes and unadjustable thermostats and batshit pizza delivery negotiations, Russia returned in the form of a candlelit feast laid out by a big-hearted woman who'd lost nearly everything when the Soviet Union collapsed, not only her plum life but also her husband and wayward son.

"Such kindness," my mother said, scooping the ladle into the borscht to fill everyone's bowl with the beet-red warmth.

A week later, they gathered up all their Arbat finds—*shapki* and *matryoshki* and other tourist baubles, and, of course, the medals from the war—and gave their suitcases to the driver, before bundling into the cab that would take them to the airport. My sister started crying.

"I don't want to leave you here," she said. She stared at my parents with conviction. "We shouldn't leave him here."

My mother said, "are you okay? Let's just take you home." Concern lined her forehead, as she leaned in to hug me again, holding tight. I could feel her invitation tugging me from the inside.

"I'll be fine," I said, lying. I didn't know how I'd be. I was grateful and flushed from their visit, their anarchic love heating up my apartment, and I didn't want them to go.

My father stood for a moment, and bear-hugged me.

"Honey," he said, "glad you're feeling better."

It took everything I had not to hop in the cab and out of this miserable existence. I waved and watched them disappear.

At customs, the security people opened their suitcase, searching for contraband. Someone lifted up the medals, squinting at them suspiciously.

"What's the problem?" my father said.

Two security guards conferred for a few minutes.

"This is forbidden," one of them said to my father.

"But this was a gift," he protested.

He tried to pull them back, but to no avail, as the evidence of Nikolai, and that meeting of our peoples, walked away and disappeared behind a security door.

A quarter century has passed. Like some crazy country-sized cicada, Russia emerged from its purported grave and back into our American lives, whirring its maddening music. Pundits talk of a Cold

War 2.0, and you can't go more than a day without another story of Russian meddling in American politics; perhaps after some decades of American meddling in Russia, the boomerang was bound to return.

Still, all this talk of Russia seems to have missed Russia itself. When I think of Russia, I remember Olya's nervous generosity. Dima's passionate intensity for poetry and the future of his country. I remember how, when I couldn't find a way to write about Russia, I found solace in translation, trying to recreate the music of a Russian poem into English, to find the right words to house all that irrepressible sound. Hundreds of poems later, I gingerly began writing my own poems again, like a stroke victim relearning to walk and talk. I haven't stopped since.

I remember, too, the Pizza Hut order, yes, and the madness of that civilization. But I keenly remember Nikolai, a man I could never know but whose gesture reached through my clouded memory and continued to shine.

Talking to my parents again, trying to get the facts exactly right, I asked my mother about the incident at customs. She remembered it differently than my father.

"Perhaps," my mother said, "they didn't actually take all of the medals."

"Where would they be?" I said.

"One may be at the bottom of my jewelry drawer," she said. "I think I may have put a couple in my shoes. I'll see if I can find them."

We have yet to find it, that peace offering in the long cold war.

PHILIP METRES was born in San Diego and grew up in the suburbs of Chicago. He earned a BA from Holy Cross College and both an MFA and PhD from Indiana University. Metres is the author of the poetry collections *To See the Earth* (2008), *A Concordance of Leaves* (2013), which won the Arab American Book Award, *Sand Opera* (2015), and *Pictures at an Exhibition* (2016), as well as numerous chapbooks. A scholar of war literature, Metres wrote the critical study *Behind the Lines: War Resistance Poetry on the American Homefront since*

1941 (2007). His work has appeared in *Best American Poetry*, and *Inclined to Speak: Contemporary Arab American Poetry* and he is the recipient of honors and awards including a National Endowment for the Arts award, a Watson Fellowship, two Ohio Arts Council Grants, and the Cleveland Arts Prize. He teaches literature and creative writing at John Carroll University in Cleveland, Ohio.

LYNN MARIE HOUSTON

My Father Sends Me a Card that Says You Are So Loved

By the time he had been in-country six months, my father
stopped calling them helicopters, referred to them instead as birds:
Yesterday, I flew out on a bird with the Captain, one of his letters reads.

Stateside, my father rode the blade and wing of war into our living room.
Once, when we played hide-and-seek, I lost him somewhere in the house.
When I finally called out, he emerged from the place I'd looked first.
A little trick I learned in Vietnam, he said.
You hide where the enemy has already searched.

But I didn't want to play the enemy. I wore his camouflage shirts
into the woods, tails tied in a knot around my waist, cuffs rolled,
the head of an eagle drooping near my elbow.
I spoke to him over an imaginary radio, *Got your six. How copy?*
I sighted targets with a bent thumb behind a rigid pointer finger.
Is it true that we can love only what we fully understand?
Roger that. I read you loud and clear.

On his first Christmas after being drafted, my father writes,
*I have adjusted from being a civilian and have accepted that I am
in Vietnam and will do my best, even though it hardly seems possible.*
The Army spent months training him to become a soldier
in an Airmobile unit—he learned to fire an M-60, rappel
from 50-feet off the ground, and set up a perimeter with trip flares.
But no one ever trained him to become a civilian again.

I've scoured my father's scrapbook of photos, read and re-read his letters,
but I've failed to understand what it means to have been born
in the shadow of this war, what it means to be loved by a man
who still calls a helicopter a bird, who still opens a trunk of green
fatigues and stares, jaw hardening, into a box full of medals.

Lynn Marie Houston holds a Ph.D. in English from Arizona State University and an MFA from Southern Connecticut State University. She is the winner of the 2018 Able Muse Poetry Contest, a recipient of an Artist Fellowship from the Connecticut Office of the Arts, and the author of three books of poetry: *The Clever Dream of Man* (winner of the Connecticut Press Club Award for Creative Work), *Unguarded* (winner of the Heartland Review Press Chapbook Contest), and *The Mauled Keeper* (winner of the National Federation of Press Women's Award for Creative Work, runner-up for the Eric Hoffman Award in Poetry, runner-up in the Cathy Smith Bowers Contest, runner-up for the New England Book Award in Poetry, and a finalist for the Montaigne Medal). She has a book of poems about helicopters and Vietnam forthcoming from Middle West Press in late 2019. For more information, please visit: lynnmhouston.com.

SARA NOVIĆ

On Late-Stage Pediatric Cardiomyopathy

Should you find yourself coming-to while being wheeled out of high school pre-calculus, it is best not to open your eyes. You will get *that* feeling, the pressure of a return to consciousness, like breathing beneath a weighted blanket. Do not make eye contact with your peers in this state. Your guard will be down; someone perceptive might see your future flickering across your dilated pupils. Feign unconsciousness for a few more seconds, until the EMTs have turned the corner.

When you return to school later, make jokes about the "episode." This will put your classmates at ease. They will give you terrible nicknames which they mean to be endearing. Accept these with a smile, internalize them, use them in reference to yourself—they are your only remaining link to the social order that was once so important.

* * *

The problem with congestive heart failure is I sometimes forget I have it. I am seventeen, heart failure is a disease for old people, and I forget. I have good days, stretches where I breathe easy and walk at a regular pace. Then I go and do something stupid—bum half a cigarette off my friend Benny behind the Dunkin' Donuts, try to chase the 37 bus, stand up too quickly—and end up back here.

At Memorial West, people know me. The ambulance driver calls ahead to let them know I'm coming, and the triage nurse high-fives me on the way in. A blistering pain ripples inside my ribcage when I move my arm, but I try not to flinch. Further down the hall, Igor, the janitor, updates me on the baseball scores. He's Ukrainian and can't pronounce his W's.

"Ey, Ven-dee, your Mets are heartbreakers this veek," he says.

"Leave Wendy alone," says the woman at Information. "She doesn't need your bad news."

"That's why I like them!" I call to Igor as I'm handed off to an orderly I've never met, who pushes me toward the elevators. But my voice shakes more than usual, and I don't know if he's heard me.

They take me straight to cardiology, where I am approximately fifty years younger than the average patient. They park my gurney alongside the nurses' station while they try to find me a room. A student tech lifts my shirt, affixing sticky electrodes up and down my torso, leaving my chest exposed, nipples prickling against the chill, sterile air. There was a point when I was ashamed of lying half-naked in public, but that seems like a long time ago now.

Behind the desk, Alisha is playing her perpetual game of Pac-Man on the computer she's supposed to use for medical records. For as many times as I've been here, I've never seen her pass the third level.

"That's cause these old people got me runnin' my ass all over this damn hospital," she says when I bring it up. She wags her head in the direction of the patient rooms, as if Pac-Man were her real job, and they were distracting her from it. She hushes my laughter. "Don't move! You'll mess up you EKG." It's only then I notice the familiar multicolored wires tentacling across my body and up to the computer. I quiet my breathing and wait while it graphs the jagged meter of my heart. The tech covers me with a gown and leaves. Alisha rips the accordion paper printout along its perforations, studies it, and calls my doctor over the loudspeaker.

* * *

Like being an expert at anything, there are insider tricks for achieving an optimal hospital stay. If you are nice to an orderly, he will give you
an extra pillow. If you make the nurses laugh, they will bring you ice chips and cans of ginger ale. If you humor the pediatric team, they will slip you hard candy under cover of secret handshakes. And there's the oxygen. Take it whenever it's offered, even if your breathing has steadied; you will get a buzz that plays nicely off any concoction already dulling your mind via the tube in the crook of your arm. Take hydromorphone whenever it's offered, too, even if you can stand the pain. It will fuck you up.

* * *

"You're a cheap date," Doctor Kingston says, when he enters the OR as my irises bloom with pain medication. He used to be much more standoffish with me, but I have worn him down. Now he makes this joke every time he is about to cut me open, and I always laugh. My heart is not strong enough to hold up under general anesthesia, so they strap me to the table and numb me instead. Today they are draining fluid from my chest cavity to ease my breathing. It is one of many procedures Dr. Kingston and I have come to call "stall tactics" when no one else is around.

"I felt that," I say when I see his hand move to make the opening below my second rib.

"Did not," he says, but he clicks the pain med button once more, just in case. As he works I watch his eyes, wide and turquoise above his surgical mask. In these moments, I willfully misinterpret his kindness for the underpinnings of an epic romance.

"You're going to miss me," I slur, emboldened. Dr. Kingston has been trying to fix me for years, and I'm sometimes ashamed he'll have to count me among his failures.

"There," he says, sliding a small hose into the incision in my side. "That should help with the pressure." I feel something bubbling inside me and the ceiling tiles swirl above my head. I squeeze my eyes shut.

He comes to check on me before he leaves for the day. Sighing, he cups my chin and presses on the wine-colored rings that have appeared beneath my eyes. I'd seen them, too, in the reflection of some glass on the way back to my room, but had been afraid to ask the nurse.

"What are they?" I say.

He is quiet.

"Just tell me."

"Your blood is pooling in concavities throughout your body as your circulatory system shuts down."

"Then what?"

"Drop in body temperature, fatigue. Loss of consciousness, depending on how stubborn you are." The ghost of a smile floats near the corner of his mouth. I smile back a little, too.

"So it won't hurt."

"Nope. This is probably the least painful part."

"How long?"

"Hard to say."

"Will you talk to my parents?"

"Always do, kiddo," he says.

* * *

At this point, your family will be a sleep-deprived, overcaffeinated knot of tension, and it is best not to expect much of them. They will worry incessantly while trying not to worry you. They will build walls; they will suddenly believe in miracles. The sicker you get, the more their concern will manifest itself as a perfumed cloud of optimism. You may find it overbearing when they arrive and congregate around
your bed. They will talk relentlessly of a cure — a transplant, implant, or procedure they have researched online.

The doctor will come around, clipboard pressed into his hipbone, and talk statistics. He will use words like "hospice" and they will float right over your parents' heads. Resist the urge to shake them. Let them have their miracles. They'll have much more time to be sad about your dying than you will.

* * *

My family arrives at dinnertime, their surplus adrenaline set loose via horseplay and shouting. I hear them down the hall at the nurses' station and feel sorry for my roommate, who is nearly a century old and has only a thin gray curtain to insulate her from my impending visitors.

"What the fuck is that?" my sister says when she takes the corner into my room. Stella, at age thirteen, has the mouth of a motorcycle gangbanger. She points to the tube protruding through a slit in my gown and draining into a canister beside the bed.

"Don't touch it!" I slap her hand away. "It's attached!" Startled, she lurches backward into my father, throwing him off balance. He flails, backhanding my mother in the face, who then knocks the IV fluid from its hooked metal pole.

"Son of a—" My mother claps her hand over the red patch on her cheek.

"Jesus H. Christ on a stick!" My father catches the IV bag and reclasps it to its stand.

"Well shit," Stella says, and runs back into the hall. I hear the rumble of the ice machine and know she is helping herself to soda and crackers from the storage closet.

"Yo Stella—you touching my stuff?" a nurse says as she passes.

"Hungry," Stella calls back with her mouth full.

I watch my father scan the room. These first minutes, his eyes readjusting to the sight of his oldest child among the landscape of whirring medical machinery, are the only times he is overtly tender.

"Your lips are looking a little blue there, girlie," he says. He sweeps my bangs aside to kiss my forehead, and I feel small again, safe with him towering above my bed.

"She's fine," my mother says. My father touches her arm, looks at her the way he does when he wants her to slow down. She leaves to find me an extra blanket, her brown pumps clacking on the linoleum.

It's not that kind of cold, I want to say. *Don't you remember? The doctor said this would happen.* Instead I reach for the playing cards Stella carries in her coat pocket. "Come on, guys," I say.

Hours later, we've collectively finished off eight cafeteria grilled cheeses, my mother has dominated the card game, and my family is packing up for the night, gathering their backpacks and laptop cases. My father searches beneath the bed for the shoes he's kicked off at some point in the evening. They promise to be back tomorrow upon completion of their daily responsibilities, which seem to occur on a plane of reality increasingly further away. My sister lingers in the doorway. Her face is sallow under the fluorescent track lighting, and I remember the bruises below my own eyes, the gathering blood that marks a turn in my condition.

"I wish you wouldn't," she says.

So do I, is another thing I don't really say.

* * *

Friendship at this stage is difficult, not because your friends are uncaring, but because you have changed. They may visit at first, call to check in, but you have unwittingly entered a long-distance relationship, and by the time you notice it, your momentum will be lost. Still there is the rare person with whom connections exist independently of time, the kind who can start a conversation one week and finish it another with nothing lost. This will be your final friend, more comforting than your family because he is not preoccupied with the unique horror of watching his own DNA dissipate. He will be a wreck when the time comes, but for now he is stable and willing to stick around as long as you do.

* * *

Benny is the kind of kid who likes smoking not because he is addicted but because he's not supposed to do it. He comes to visit in the middle of the night because he gets off on breaking protocol. When I was in elementary school I'd slink up two floors to the pediatric oncology wing and have wheelchair races with the casualties of childhood cancer—I remember the thrill of navigating the deserted hallways without permission. So I leave Benny to his
tiptoeing. I don't tell him the nurses would let him in anyway if I asked them to.

He slides into the shadows of my room as if he has been inching against the wall down the entire corridor, and I laugh picturing what must have been the most conspicuous sneaking in the history of visiting-hour breeches.

"Hey, creep," he whispers. "How's it going?" He kicks off his sneakers and lays down in my bed, squeezing himself against the bedrail. His fingers brush mine. "You're cold."

"I'm fabulous," I say.

"You're high." He averts his gaze from my lie, changes the subject. "Casey Walker got suspended for blowing Pete Hinds in the art room—*in* the kiln—yesterday."

"I miss all the good stuff."

"I missed you," he says, and leans in. I wish I had powdered away my black eyes.

"Me too," I say, mid-kiss. I like the way his lips stretch across mine when he smiles.

We have kissed in other places, under circumstances better than these—on the big hill in the state park, under the stairs in the science hallway—and I position myself among those backdrops now instead of here. We never bothered with the terminology of coupledom, though our friends have more than once declared us "together." Now I am glad we never really dated, never gave ourselves the opportunity to bicker and break up.

We talk about where we might apply to college, about how he'll be an eccentric architect and design us strange houses with too many staircases, or how, when we're really old, we'll meet on one another's stoops to take our daily walks. His eyes glow green like traffic lights, and I let myself go, for a moment, into an existence where we are seventy and Benny smokes a pipe, our lives culminating in a series of completely unexceptional events. It is this world, the one I've not yet been to, that I will miss the most.

"It's okay, you know," Benny says before he leaves. His voice is smaller than usual.

"What?"

He stuffs his hands in his pockets, stares at his Vans. "To…not get better."

No one has ever said this out loud, and at first the words seem leaded, falling from my mind directly into my stomach. Then another feeling, a warmth welling up in my throat: relief.

"Thank you," I say, though I wish for something stronger.

In the darkest hours of the morning, I begin shivering. I try to stop. I focus on the little moan my roommate croaks out when she reaches through sleep for a deep breath. It doesn't help. I shake all over, and I don't know if it's from cold or fear.

* * *

In the end, your body will know what to do. It will be methodical—a factory foreman adhering to procedure, the deliberate shutdown of systems. Do not panic. Do not micromanage. Try not to be bitter that your roommate is recovering and will go home tomorrow. It's not her fault you are sick.

Lie still. Wait for the light your friends from the cancer ward saw the nights you remained by their bedsides to see them through. If you can't find it, don't worry; it was probably just a reaction to the chemo, brain cells dissolving under the weight of poison and fatigue. As with our beginnings, there will rarely be anything extraordinary about the endings. Everyone will go eventually, some in this same bed. When you start to feel tired, close your eyes. It will be easier for everyone later, if they don't have to do it for you.

Pretend you are small and have been sent to bed early while the household remains lit and alive beneath you. The television will continue to flash; the refrigerator will engage its cyclical hum without you. Take solace in the fact that at least these things you're not seeing are commonplace. Submit to the weight of sleep. Allow yourself to believe you aren't missing anything.

* * *

The sun's come up and the nurses are darting around my room, unplugging this and adjusting that, their rubber shoes squeaking as they spring from one machine to the next. They declare me unconscious. They yell to the receptionist to call my mother. I want to tell them they're moving much too quickly, that if they'd just slow down they'd notice the flit of my eyelashes, the twitch of my hand, and know I was still listening. But my eyelids hang heavy and my jaw feels disconnected, so I say nothing. I hear something familiar, the rattle of air pushing through faulty piping. I recognize it as a sound I've heard here before—a patient's breathing in her final hours—and realize it's resonating up from within me.

My family enters quietly. I know it's too early for them to be finished with their normal routines, that they've gotten the phone call and rushed over. This time I don't feel guilty for disrupting their schedules, am not irked by their desperate hopefulness. The scrape of wood against tile as they pull chairs close around my bed calms me.

They reminisce about things we used to do, then stop talking and take turns holding my hand. When I get Stella's, I squeeze it hardest, running my thumb against the tips of her unmarred fingers.

It is the first time I can remember all of them being completely silent. This, more than the coursing ache in my body, confirms the brevity of my time remaining.

I shuffle through mental archives, seeking something beautiful to fill these final moments. The ocean, Benny's and my first kiss, snow flurries in the days before Christmas. But everything I conjure up is interrupted by the schoolyard of my earliest childhood, and eventually I let the memory overtake me. The school, a dull brick box, sits atop a hill. I stand on the edge of the playground, the space where the gravel and tar meet browning grass, my hands behind my back, fingers entwined in the fence that surrounds the property. A bell rings, signaling the end of recess, and my classmates dash up to the double doors of the school. As they run, they drop the red rubber dodgeballs they've been so enchanted with, and the balls roll down the slanted blacktop, a scarlet wave rushing toward chain-link.

Somewhere in the distance I hear the angry buzz of alarms. I watch the other children form neat lines and file back into the building. The dodgeballs recoil, expelling their final caches of energy, then rest motionless against the fence. I exhale.

SARA NOVIĆ is the author of *Girl at War* (Random House), which won an American Library Association Alex Award and has been translated into more than a dozen languages. Her next book, a collection of short biographies of American immigrants from all of the world's 195 countries, is forthcoming in 2019. She's an Assistant Professor of Creative Writing at Stockton University in New Jersey.

LUCY SATTLER

Artist's Statement

Since I was a little girl, I dreamt of joining the Air Force. I lived not far from a base, and grew up listening to Herc's flying overhead. I always knew one day I would join them.

I began sewing at the age of four, learning from my mother and grandmother, and textiles have always seemed as much a natural part of life as the RAAF did. Quilts are warm, familiar and tactile – they remind us of home, comfort, and love; words not often associated with military service.

The juxtaposition of textiles with striking military imagery is often confronting for viewers. Drawn to the mixture of fabrics and textures, people move closer to inspect in disbelief. As they are challenged visually to revisit their assumptions of quilts and textile art, they are also challenged to rethink how they view service, and the impact it has on lives.

Military families undergo their own set of unique challenges, and while life within the service can appear confronting and alien to 'civvies', many aspects of military family life are identical, just with a few changes of costume.

Two of these works are from our annual Australian Anzac Day celebrations (*Aled at the March* and *On The Train, Anzac Day 2014*), one of the most important days in a military family's calendar, where the younger members get to watch Mum and/or Dad march in the big parade.

Unlike the sterilized recruitment imagery or carefully curated media released by Defence, these images are personal, intimate and unfiltered, giving the audience a glimpse of what life is truly like for those of us who serve.

LUCY SATTLER was born in the UK, but raised in Sydney, Australia. She now lives in tropical Far North Queensland and continues to make quilts and textiles from her studio. At the age of 17, Sattler left home and went to the Australian Defence Force Academy with the Royal Australian Air Force. After graduation she became a RAAF Air Traffic Control Officer, controlling aircraft from Blackhawks to C17's, and even Air Force One. She left the RAAF to raise her children, and now works as a professional artist with a Graduate Diploma in Fine Arts from James Cook University. Sattler has exhibited work and won awards throughout Australia and overseas, and has had several public commissions for her work.

Soldier On

Ten Shoes for Ten Feet

Work Ready

On the Train, Anzac Day

Aled at the March

Kelly

Soldier On (Detail)

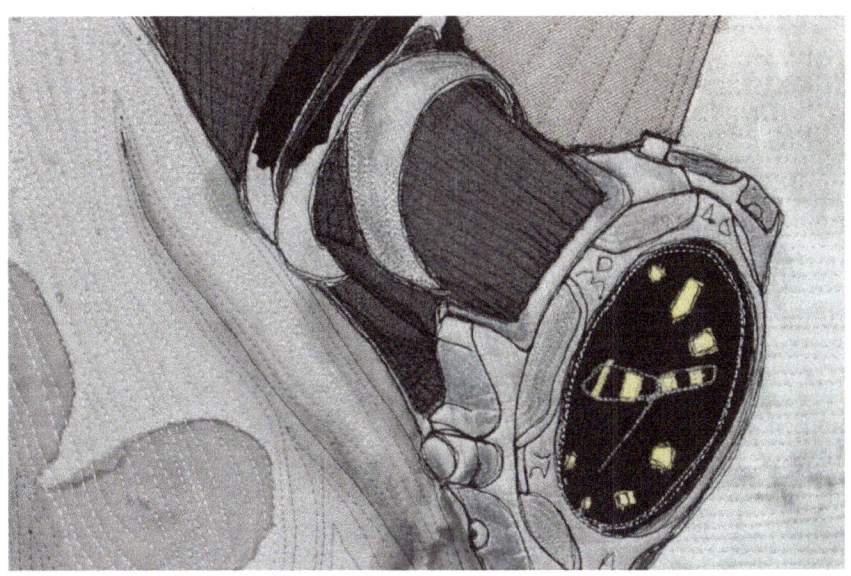

Work Ready (Detail)

DREW PHAM

Because of George H.W. Bush, I Thought Smart Bombs Were a Good Thing

like the American Dream
and McDonald's Happy Meals
and democracy
and a big house
and the mortgage that comes with it
and grocery stores with enough rice to feed a village
and meat—not just on Tết, like Mom during the war—but every day
and G.I. Joes from the cartoons
of which the white boy next door had boxes full
and took for granted
but Dad thought were too expensive
so I got sack loads of green and tan army men
that came with flags
for each side like Old Glory for the good guys
and Germany's
and once after the Gulf War, Iraq's
but most often Việt Nam's
yet this was peace
and we had all the things my parents never had during the war
so Dad voted Republican because it was Nixon that ended it after all—

though
    Saigon
        fell
            under
                Ford
            and
      I
    barely
  remember
Operation Desert Shield
    but don't you think it's the bad kind of mixed metaphor
      when a shield becomes a storm?
          I do remember NBC or ABC covering it
            and General Schwarzkopf saying
        I'm now going to show you a picture of the luckiest man in Iraq
          and Mom cringed
          and didn't want to look
        and turned away just like she did during Bosnia
      but Dad bought me the *Gulf War 4 Pack VHS Set*
  no shit that was the title
and I was only four
but when I turned five it's all I ever watched because Barney never did
bring on a Vietnamese kid like me
so I was obsessed
with machines like the M1 Abrams Main Battle Tank
and the F4 Phantom II in its Wild Weasel configuration
and the B-52 Stratofortress
both of which Mom recognized from her war
which is why it was all so hard to watch
but Dad said they had stealth jets with smart bombs
so It wouldn't be like it was
in Việt Nam—this was back when he still told himself he loved her
    before he went back home after Clinton opened the country
    before he took another lover over there and brought her back here
    before my mom broke a dustpan over his head when he called her a whore
    before my aunt spotted him with that woman in an Atlantic City casino
    before he left for good.

When you believe that there's such a thing as a smart bomb you can believe in such a thing as a good soldier even though your mother never believed the words *good* and *soldier* should ever be conjoined because what is good about a soldier drafting a seventeen-year-old to go and fight in Cambodia when the war should've been over years ago? She left with her whole family and they came here where the grocery stores dazzled her and there was so much promise and she had her degree and her parents were math teachers but they still cleaned fast food joints after hours because all they were in the end were just another source of cheap labor and her brother died anyway but in a lovers spat and she worked and worked and by some sick cosmic joke she married a man from the other side (it was a civil war) and got a job in the defense industry and gave birth to two boys and a girl and both boys joined the Army and she went to Kuwait after the invasion (the second go-around) and she had to do all that just so she could qualify for a mortgage on a house she'd end up selling anyway just so she could have a little of all that food that would get thrown out if she didn't buy it before the sell by date just so she could worry about another pair of boys about to go to off to fight.

The day George H. W. Bush dies they fly the flag at half mast at
        Brooklyn College as if the Drug War never happened
                my Twitter friends—they're well meaning people—say:
                      now that was a president
                          look at his poise
                              his civility
                                    his fucking socks
but they've never fired an M120's M395 Precision Guided Mortar Munition
at a target
only to miss by a full kilometer
—the Colonel really freaked at that one
and how surgical is a smart bomb if the kill radius is seventy meters?
and how many schools
and roads
and toilets
and hospitals
could you build for one Tomahawk Cruise Missile?

I tell my friends that I want to write a poem
titled, "Because of George H.W. Bush, I thought Smart Bombs Were a Good Thing"
with the lines,
> *In hell, I hope the GBU-Paveway IIs are precise*
> *enough to pass*
> *through your asshole*
> *for an eternity with*
> *surgical precision*

but the kill
radius of a stanza like that would be smaller than
the real thing
so I say let's remember the dead
presidents and the future
dead presidents for all the things we thought were good
like money
for college and
a guarantee not to be vaporized on your way to school
and
that white picket fence Dad lost in the bankruptcy
and how those things made Mom
forget that
no matter
how hard
she tried to save my uncle
she still had to clean out his bedroom when he died
she feels it today
like shrapnel, from a bomb dropped decades ago,
lodged in her side
and mine.

Drew Pham is an adjunct English lecturer and Brooklyn-based writer. He deployed to Afghanistan in 2010 with the 10th Mountain Division.

DAVID MORRIS

Pro Patria

Throughout my youth, my father could always be counted upon for a motivational slogan. In times of crisis, these nuggets of wisdom would sprout from his mouth, forming a kind of pithy patchwork for our years together. Later, these phrases became power words, mantras that I would say to myself at certain moments. Without realizing it I came to believe in them, organize my life around them.

"Early bird gets the worm."
"Gotta make hay while the sun shines."
"Sometimes you just need a bigger hammer."
"Tough times don't last, tough people do."

My father was not a reader of books and never claimed to be the second coming of Vince Lombardi, but he'd done well for himself. He'd been raised on a beef cattle ranch in Eastern Oregon and after a tour in the navy in Vietnam, he'd started a successful real estate business in San Diego that allowed him to live in a manner that was the envy of his brothers and sisters who had all remained in Oregon. Despite his comparative affluence, he hated the trappings of American wealth and sneered at the mere mention of golf, never joined a country club, rarely took vacations and put in twelve hour days, six days a week at the office. Sundays were spent at the gym. His major concession to luxury was the brand-new BMW 5-series he purchased every other year, always in gun-metal. Hard work, free enterprise and the US military were the only things he had any faith in, as evidenced by his three marriages. Grit, perseverance, not being a candy ass. These were the major themes of my childhood.

Wherever I went, people seemed to hammer on these themes. (Did I choose the path, or did the path choose me?) Something in my face seemed to speak to my teachers and coaches, urging them to lean harder into me. I had and still have an excruciatingly readable face and I think my teachers took my expressions as a challenge to their authority: I was a piece of leather begging to be tanned. My father was only one of many leather workers, but naturally it is his hands that I remember best. Later in life, I would remind myself that he'd known only the ranch growing up. There was no beach time or cable television waiting for him at the end of the day—only an early turn-in and early rise for the next work day. His life was a monument to the most basic of pioneer rhythms, the never-ending work cycle, the cattle drive to the railhead, the hunt for deer and elk. To deviate from these immortal habits was to invite chaos.

Like a lot of navy men, my father stayed in San Diego after the war, raising my brother and I with my mom in a tract house in a military suburb called Poway, a name that meant "the end of the valley" in the local Indian dialect. The sea was miles away but during big winter swells, the salty air would drift up the valley and park itself over the stands of oak and eucalyptus trees, making the area feel like a lost neighborhood of San Francisco. The Miramar air station was down the road and most of our neighbors were pilots or retired pilots or Marine officers who'd served in Vietnam. Our next door neighbor, a man named Ernst, served as a technical advisor on *Top Gun* and among the many photographs lining the walls of his den was a picture of him with Tom Cruise.

Every August the family went to the Miramar Air Show and watched the Blue Angels, the Navy's aerobatic squadron perform. Crowds estimated in the hundreds of thousands lined the tarmac to watch the Blue Angels perform stunts with names like the "Delta Break Out," the "Diamond Half-Cuban Eight" and the "Double Farvel." Afterward, my brother Dan and I would chat up the pilots and take photographs posing in front of our favorite jets. Mine was the F-15C

Eagle, built by McDonnell Douglas. My brother preferred the Lockheed SR-71 Blackbird, which held a number of speed records and was, by some definitions, technically a spacecraft because it flew so high. We spent entire weeks in the garage during the summer laboring over plastic models of F-15s, SR-71s, F-18s, and F-4 Phantoms, painting their wings with tiny brushes made in Italy. One of our neighbors down the street had recently been accepted to the Air Force Academy and being good Poway kids, we steadfastly maintained the superiority of the Navy and Marine Corps over the Air Force, or as we called it, the "Chair Force."

My brother and I attended the excellent public schools a couple miles from home and there we played football and wrestled and mostly got good grades, though my brother was a star of the classroom in a way that I never would be. Because he had three inches and twenty pounds on me, he was sought by the football coaching staff, even though I had played Pop Warner ball and he had not. Dan would go on to graduate third in his class, just out of the spotlight, yet retaining a preternatural ability to please adults simply with his presence. By contrast, I was a bit of a fuck-up, good in English, indomitable in History (I once corrected a teacher about the nature of the landings at Omaha Beach), but comically bad at Math. The Science Department viewed me with a sort of sighing disappointment, as if they had been given charge of Newton's half-wit cousin.

As soon as my brother and I were old enough—twelve in my case—we were taken on month-long backpacking trips to Oregon and the Sierra Nevada led by my father, my uncle Mark and his wife Jane. The goal, my father explained, was to backpack around the base of Denali in Alaska after my senior year of high school. My father had grown up the hard way and he seemed to look upon these expeditions as being central to our upbringing, even though in truth, my brother and I preferred to think of ourselves as ocean people. The idea that these trips—where we averaged ten miles a day at high altitude—would exhaust most adult American males would only occur me years later when I would watch to my delight as one after another of my fellow officer candidates passed out and were snatched up by waiting ambulances on a perfectly level piece of trail in the Quantico woods, never to be heard from again. By the time I was a junior in high school I had summited Mount Whitney twice by two different routes and hiked the entirety of the John Muir Trail from north to south. Dan and I grew up tough and while he was clearly the better student, I was the better pain sponge, a fact that no doubt played into my decision to join the Marine Corps without really thinking about it too much.

The spell of High Americana seemed to break once my brother graduated from high school and went off to college in Berkeley, leaving me unattended, alone in our too-perfect house with only my Dad, his real estate business that seemed to leave him with more money than he knew how to reasonably spend and his new second wife, a recent émigré from Houston and the daughter of an oil scion. For reasons that remain obscure even to me, my grades plummeted and by the end of my junior year there was talk of me being sent to a boys' academy in Eastern Oregon that doubled as a working cattle ranch. Later, through a convoluted series of events involving a former regent that my stepmother had tended to in his hour of mortal need when she worked as a nurse at the Anderson Medical Center, it was arranged for me to attend Texas A&M as a cadet, provided I attended a local junior college the summer before fall classes began and maintained a "B"-average. Thus the military and eventually the Marine Corps became a kind of reform school for me.

Texas A&M taught me the beauty of repetition, the transcendence of mindlessness. As cadets, we rose every day at the same time and ran the same three miles around campus, chanting the same words to the same war songs. ("One, Two, Three, Four, Every day I Pray For War…") I learned to appreciate the beauty of identical things, until I yearned to become identical myself, to think of myself as a piece of a machine, the working member of a team. For weeks, the hot clear weather was unvarying; I wore the same shade of khaki that cadets had worn a hundred years before, the co-eds wore maroon ribbons in their hair, the cadet band played the same songs in the same order every evening before dinner, ending always with the "Aggie War Hymn." The day ended with taps being played by the A&M bugle corps. More than once these notes, played by four buglers at the far ends of the cadet quad, brought me to tears.

Repetition gave way to discipline and my grades rose. I liked the process, the feeling of control it gave me. Being a cadet had given me a sense of mastery over my life, though I could feel that the Corps of Cadets wasn't enough. The spring of my junior year, my roommate was kicked out of school for smoking pot. Alone in my barracks room, I flipped out and started attending meetings of the campus philosophy club. Discussing existentialism, the ethics of suicide, and the cult of Dionysius while wearing a uniform gave me the feeling of being high in some way. I began to feel like a secret agent. On the outside I was an automaton, a khaki-clad robot, but inside I was a revolutionary who listened to Sonic Youth, read Nietzsche and flirted with vegetarianism. Within me I hoped to contain all human contradiction, the wisdom that existed between opposites. I began to think of human truth as a bird in flight, a shadow that could be glimpsed only by those who kept their eyes pinned to the skies.

In our quarters, we were allotted a single 3X5 card of "personal space" on the cork boards over our desks. Over my desk was an index card with the words my father had spoken years before:

TOUGH TIMES DON'T LAST
TOUGH PEOPLE DO

This truism stood vigil over my studies for three years before I began to see certain conceptual flaws in it. The sentiment had a certain appeal to it, naturally, but the idea that brainless endurance was the key to life was self-destructive, almost self-immolating when you actually thought about it. It began to gnaw at me. In my short time on earth, I'd already met a number of stubborn idiots who seemed to live by the light of this platitude. By the time my junior year arrived, I'd come to accept the essential idiocy of the saying but I left the 3X5 card up on my corkboard as a symbol, a bullshit relic of my youth that had nevertheless kept me in good stead. It was a sinister thing to discover at such an age—that an axiom, a law of your upbringing could be proven bogus once you really looked at it.

I had accomplished a number of things in Texas—I was a solid citizen, I was on my way to a college degree, I had a future—but inside I was going mad. I liked the structure the Corps of Cadets had given me but I had to leave. And yet I had nowhere else to go. It started with a book—an immense volume on the Occult, assigned reading for a course on the philosophy of religion. Reading it was terrifying. Between its covers was every forbidden idea I'd ever heard of. The problem presented by the book was simple: it was evil and yet I enjoyed it. I liked reading about witchcraft, numerology, tarot, human sacrifice and Kabbalah. I liked dwelling on the black arts that the Catholic Church had spent centuries trying to eradicate. Satanism and Aleister Crowley. Alchemy and paganism. The sacred feminine and yoga. Astrology and human fate. Schizophrenia and the divine. The role that the planet Mercury played in the rise of the United States of America. I read some chapters so many times the pages began to fall out. I became fascinated by words like apophenia, divination, arcana, calcination, gematria, Hesed and Geburah. Walking to class I would repeat these words over and over again, the taps on my polished black oxfords keeping time.

An almost carnal thrill accompanied the reading of this book. What was wrong with me? Was I going mad? How did I reconcile these ideas with the sense of myself as a clean-cut, football-loving American boy? I became seriously depressed. Yet I went to the library and checked out more books on the subject. Many things had been published since the appearance of the original volume. The Sixties and the reaction to the war in Vietnam had unleashed a torrent of interest, new publications and even board games relating to the Occult. New subcultures appeared, whole societies in the Pacific Northwest seemed to have been called into being in this time, all reaching towards some new level of connection with the infinite.

I became more fascinated, more depressed.

Finally, my orders for Officer Candidate School at Quantico appeared. It was a test every neophyte had to undergo. When the secretary in the military sciences building handed them to me, I was stricken. Feeling like a condemned man, I went for a long walk around campus, visiting as many shrines to fallen students as I could take in before evening formation. When I got back to my room in the barracks, I pinned my orders beneath the 3X5 card on my cork board.

I stayed in my room for weeks, leaving only for formations, re-reading my occult books, mixed with histories of the Vietnam War, wondering what it all meant. I got to the point where I could recite the

Kabbalah Tree of Life from Kether to Malkuth, along with every major American operation during the war from Harvest Moon to Rolling Thunder. I flirted with the idea of calling it all off, of transferring to San Diego State. I had two years of college under my belt. There were places I could go. Things I could do. I fantasized about becoming a surfer and wandering the world in search of waves. I imagined myself on a beach in Latin America somewhere, testing myself in a different way, against a different kind of dream, like some of my friends from high school were doing. There was a wave that broke off of Baja California rumored to be the biggest in the world under certain conditions. It seemed like a new kind of big game hunting and I'd kept an old issue of National Geographic with an article about Baja in it stashed in my desk. The fact that I'd stolen it out of the university library only doubled the illicit thrill. Sometimes without thinking, I'd find myself leafing through it, not really looking at the pictures.

Then my airplane tickets for Quantico arrived in the company mailbox. I ignored them for a week, hoping they'd vanish of their own accord and that I'd been relieved of my calling by some clerical error. Finally, some dutiful cadet noticed them collecting dust and shoved them under my barracks door. Seeing the manila folder with my name on it laying diagonally across the floor, my heart began beating like a horse trying to break out of its stall.

Quitting seemed like it was the wiser move, long-term, but I'd given too much to back out now. I could feel the logic of momentum working on me. I could be identical. I knew it. I could fit in. I could be like the others on the outside but a rebel on the inside, an artist in uniform like T.E. Lawrence or J.F.C. Fuller. I was fit. I could run three miles in under seventeen minutes. I could disassemble and re-assemble an M16 blindfolded. I could read a topographic map, use a lensatic compass. I liked the idea of losing myself in the service, having a uniform to hide behind. Dropping out now felt like what bailing to Canada had been to a previous generation. I knew that a part of me would wonder what I had given up by backing out of the dare; the dare that asked, can you take it? Can you make it as a Marine? Can you go to a war? I feared the embarrassment that would ensue if I quit. It was in the nature of my upbringing to stick things out, as I had stuck out playing football, even though I'd hated it after the first season. More than anything, I feared appearing weak in my father's eyes, and my weeks alone in the barracks with only my histories to keep me company had revealed to me a simple truth—my life was meaningless without the military.

DAVID MORRIS is a former Marine infantry officer and author of *The Evil Hours* (Houghton Mifflin Harcourt) and *Storm on the Horizon* (Free Press). He worked in Iraq from 2004 to 2007 as a reporter for *Salon* and the *Virginia Quarterly Review*. His writing has appeared in *The New Yorker*, *Slate*, *The Daily Beast*, *The Los Angeles Times* and elsewhere. Morris was awarded a creative nonfiction fellowship from the National Endowment for the Arts as well as residencies at The MacDowell Colony and the Norman Mailer Writers Colony in Provincetown, Massachusetts. He is a graduate of Texas A&M and UC Irvine.

MARLÉNE ZADIG

Soldier's Joy

The light was especially kind that morning. It charged the threads of spider silk adorning the hundred-year-old magnolia branches—bare and antlered from drought—reaching just outside the second-story window. The gilded strands swayed and glinted in the breeze, seeming almost harmonic, like the strings of a wild and rustic instrument awaiting their woodland maestro. A fog rolled in and they were gone; it passed by and they shone brightly once more. Helga's mood plummeted and rose accordingly, and she spent the duration of the morning alone in a rocking chair waiting to be shot down by a cloud.

The child eventually woke from his morning nap and crawled up into Helga's lap. She kissed him beside the mounded rough patch bulging through his forehead up near his hairline. It was round like a coin at its base and jutted out with a small domed top like a nascent mushroom, but the nub of it was hard and calcified, like a horn. It was in fact a horn, according to x-rays, though whether it would eventually curve up and out like a rhinoceros, grow straight and spiraled like a unicorn, or perhaps emerge in some other pattern entirely remained unknown. As far as anyone could tell her, there was no verifiable precedent for a human child born with a bony spur fused to the skull that defied any and all attempts at inhibition. It grew and grew.

At first, Helga billed the rough patch as merely a birthmark when they were out together at playgroups or the park, but recently it had begun to elongate and take shape. Despite the boy's bowl cut with thick black hair fringed down to his eyebrows, the prong now poked through most of Helga's efforts at disguise. The other parents had been almost gleefully indulgent of the growth when it had been small and localized, employing that syrupy, self-congratulatory approach commonly reserved for the mentally disabled, but now they avoided the mother-son pair as if they were contagious.

"Marshmallow mix?" her son Jamie asked while nestled into her bosom on the rocking chair as they gazed out the window together.

"Only if you promise not to tell anyone I gave you marshmallows," she replied, to a solemn nod from Jamie. The snack in question was comprised of dry Cheerios with pretzels, raisins, and very few miniature marshmallows tossed in as a small treat. Though it pleased Helga to provide Jamie with such tiny indulgences, she feared the repercussions if anyone at the clinic or the county knew she was feeding her two-year-old even miniscule amounts of marshmallows. Though she knew there was no law against feeding young children reasonably small quantities of candy, she also knew that children had been removed from their parents in this country for far less. It gave her little comfort that she was doing everything by the book. The book they used seemed to be updated continuously and composed in invisible ink.

The pregnancy had been unintended. Helga was a war widow who'd taken frequent lovers—many of them strangers—in the months following the sudden death of her beloved husband. The doctors had requested a DNA sample from the father of her son, but she couldn't provide one, and this led them to view her with greater suspicion than they'd already had to begin with. They interrogated her repeatedly regarding any potential behaviors that could have been associated with birth-defects, specifically drug and alcohol abuse, none of which she'd touched while pregnant. She understood they were only doing it to try to figure out what was happening in the absence of clear explanations. Still, ever since those probing questions, she'd instinctually fashioned a cloak of enhanced probity that she felt would've never been required of just your average single mother: no alcohol for her (even in moderation), only organic foods for Jamie, no babysitters. Now she was the single mother of a child with an unusual mutation, and she sensed that the two of them would need to proactively assuage others' concerns as a matter of survival.

Though she'd drifted on a current of unease ever since the growth was identified, Helga knew definitively that they were truly in jeopardy when she received the eviction notice two weeks before. Their landlord was a Polish woman named Agnieska who'd once boasted to acquaintances about renting the upstairs apartment in her split-level duplex to the wife of a war hero. Agnieska was a conservative Catholic and now a naturalized American citizen, and she knew that close proximity to decorated military veterans brought with it a certain social cachet, especially in patriotic Suisun City so near to the air force base. Her own husband had been a veteran back in their home country, but he'd since died of alcoholism, and it was felt that Helga's tenancy would help exalt the woman's status out of her base substrate of sustained shame.

Agnieska had turned a blind eye to the obvious signs of Helga's fornication (as evidenced by her frequent overnight male guests) and warmly welcomed the arrival of the baby even though he would be born out of wedlock. She had been unable to produce children of her own as a result of an early, necessary hysterectomy, and she'd declared herself little Jamie's surrogate grandmother well in advance of his birth.

Now that it was impossible to conceal that the child possessed a bizarre, vaguely heretical deformity, and that Helga was refusing to follow the advice of medical and psychological clinicians to have the horn surgically removed, Agnieska had expressed in person (in advance of the formal notice) that the duo would need to vacate the apartment within thirty days or else she would fabricate some evidence of neglect and report Helga to child protective services.

"I'm not saying he can't have the surgery," Helga insisted to everyone with an opinion on the matter—which was indeed everyone, including Agnieska, "just that we need to wait until Jamie is old enough to decide for himself. What if we put him through this traumatic operation and it grows back anyway? What if it causes him excruciating chronic pain? What if he likes having a horn? Who are we to choose?

Maybe I'm being naïve, but no one can make the case that it's actually hurting anything."

Agnieska had taken the stance, however, that the horn was emblematic of grave sin. "The only human figures with horns are satyrs and Satan," she decried.

"But those are both two-horned creatures," Helga pointed out, reluctantly condescending to the debate. "Isn't this more in the vein of a unicorn? Is that not a noble creature of antiquity?"

The woman snorted. "If this were a unicorn situation, he wouldn't have found his way to the likes of you, child. No, I'll not be associated with evil, and I'll certainly not live under the same roof as its spawn. You must go away."

Helga had been a runaway herself in her youth and had no home to go back to. She'd been conceived as cheap labor and born into a family of six other children on a sheep farm outside of Dixon. At sixteen she hopped a train west to Oakland, procuring work with a fake ID as a live-in nanny to a family of middling academics in the hills above UC Berkeley. After a few years, she'd saved enough to pay for Early Childhood Education units at the city college in order to obtain a steady job working as a preschool aide so she could afford her own place and move out from under the groaning body of the history professor who paid her to be his mistress when she wasn't caring for his three cherubic children.

Helga met her husband while still living in Berkeley. He was on an ROTC scholarship to Cal; she was regularly venturing out with her preschool charges on walking fieldtrips to campus in the hopes that the great importance of higher educational institutions would seep into their collective developing subconscious and leave a permanent mark. Their first encounter was a calamity: he crashed into her while navigating a sharp turn on his scooter around some overgrown boxwoods, and though she was only mildly scuffed up and bruised by the impact, he'd insisted on missing his calculus class to escort Helga and her flock all the way back to preschool to be sure she hadn't sprained anything vital in the collision. Love came easily after all that.

* * *

Helga examined Jamie's ruddy features in the kitchen as she compiled the ingredients for his snack mix. Though she knew the child couldn't be the offspring of her late husband, she nevertheless reveled in their uncanny resemblance.

"Juice?" Jamie asked. Same chestnut eyes.

"No juice with marshmallow mix, but I'll get you some water, okay?"

Same mop of hair. Same plucky spirit. It was as if her son's conception had transcended the grave.

Her husband's name was Juan but he went by Johnny, and they'd eloped after six weeks of passionate petting. She fell in love with his dignity and chivalry, both of which somehow remained intact even when he drank heavily, which wasn't especially often. Helga followed him to various flight training posts around the country, and eventually back to the greater Bay Area to Travis Air Force Base, from which he was subsequently deployed in support of Operation Inherent Resolve against Islamic State ground forces. Johnny—Johnny Quest among his squadron—flew Apache helicopters that rained down Hellfire missiles until the IS eventually stung back with an RPG and he crashed down somewhere in the bowels of Mesopotamia, exploding on impact. He'd missed reaching the end of his tour by less than a week.

Helga succumbed to the news with a deep, silent grief and then proceeded to sleep with nearly all of the members of her late husband's squadron once they returned from war. It became a sort of ritual for each of them to rotate checking in on Johnny's widow to pay their respects and then lie with her before they went home. She would cook them dinner and would later initiate the lovemaking by saying, "Johnny would've wanted us to do this in his memory." It made no sense to any of them, including Helga, but everyone was terribly sad and this felt better than not having sex while still being terribly sad. In that way, the ritual became a kind of sacrament.

When she'd worked her way through all the men in the squadron and they stopped coming by as often—many of them had wives and girlfriends of their own—she took up pole dancing at a local strip club. She did this not for the money (she had a widow's pension), but because it gave her an outlet to perform her grief in a way that she wasn't able to do in her normal life.

"Helga the Horrible" was her dance persona, complete with Viking-inspired lingerie and realistically artificial blond braids. When Helga danced, she often wept, and she would use the braids to wipe away the tears. She was the most heartbreaking Viking stripper there ever was, and the regulars adored her.

When Helga became pregnant with Jamie, she didn't question it at all; it had seemed to her a foretold thing. She quit working at the club and reenrolled in community college, hoping to earn enough credits to become a lead preschool teacher, eager to eventually teach with her son by her side. She devoted her gestation to preparing her nest and her life for the arrival of her unborn child.

Jamie emerged a pink and healthy seven-and-a-half pounds and passed the neonatal checkup with flying colors except for the peculiar button on his forehead. To the naked eye, the patch was pocked with fissures like a pumice stone and looked almost porous. Under a magnifying glass, the blemish revealed such wonderful divots and craters and reminded Helga of the surface of the moon. Later x-rays revealed that it was in fact bone protruding through the skin, but it seemed only minorly anomalous and eventually fixable until it became clear after many more months that the stub was steadily growing outward—that it was active and alive.

The doctors then began characterizing the growth almost as a cancer, though there was no evidence of malignancy, and psychologists warned of the boy becoming an outcast if nothing was done. The child seemed perfectly healthy by all other measures, but the fact that Helga refused aggressive treatment spurred whispers of the potential for her to be ruled unfit as his mother, for the state to remove the child from her care and treat him against her wishes. She abruptly stopped taking him to doctors and was contemplating moving someplace more remote and more open-minded to difference—perhaps the Santa Cruz mountains—when she received a second eviction notice from her landlord Agnieska earlier that morning under her door.

"Just five marshmallows, today, okay?" Helga said, loading up a melamine bowl with the snack mix. "Let's count them together as I put them in—"

"1," "1,"
"2," "2,"
"3," "3,"
"4," "4,"
"5!" "5!"

"Good counting!" she said, reaching over to ruffle his hair, which defied all attempts at being mussed. It was broom-straight and always collapsed right back into place on its own.

The child munched on his snack, leaving the marshmallows for last, while Helga washed dishes at the sink. A sudden loud knock at the door interrupted them both. Helga stepped away from the sink but left the water running to mask the sound of their movements in the apartment.

The knocking continued and rose in impertinence as Helga held a finger to her lips and refused to answer. She took Jamie's hand and helped him off the dining chair to retreat to the bedroom at the front of the apartment. She closed and locked the bedroom door and hauled her wardrobe in front of it, then tied some sheets together and improvised a baby carrier around her shoulders from a long wrap skirt in case it became necessary to leave through the window. Though Jamie seemed unperturbed, Helga hummed a jaunty tune—"Soldier's Joy" was the first to come to mind—to help keep him (or perhaps just her) calm while the knocking persisted with still no announcement to identify the knocker. If it had been Agnieska or someone from the county, they would have said so, but whoever it was wasn't interested in making their intentions known.

"Let's play a quiet game, shall we?" Helga said and Jamie nodded. "We'll play a quiet game of hide-and-seek where we hide and no one finds us, and then we win."

They lingered on the bed together for a long ten minutes while the knocking reverberated through the flat and ten more minutes after it had subsided, Helga continuing to hum softly while Jamie traced his tiny fingers over the wooden buttons of her oversized sweater. The buttons had been crafted from the sanded cross-sections of thin branches and he'd once referred to them as tree-cookies. Helga and Jamie looked out on the denuded canopy of the old magnolia but the light had changed by then, aimed now from more directly overhead, and they could no longer see those strands of spider silk incandescing in the warm sun. The filaments had all but disappeared.

"Is this because of my pointer?" Jamie asked of the knocking at the door once the apartment fell silent. This was the neutral term Helga had invented to render the growth more benign in her son's imagination in contrast to others' barely concealed alarm.

"No, sweetie, it's just someone being naughty."

They passed the remainder of the day inside the apartment and only prepared to venture out to the park late into the following morning once Helga decided there was enough foot traffic on the street. She wanted to be assured of the presence of witnesses.

She went to check the weather on her phone and noticed an email from one of the men in Johnny's former squadron, Nathaniel, the one she'd spent the most time with in the months following Johnny's death. She almost never received emails that weren't promotional in nature, so she opened it right away.

"Mrs. JQ—have you seen this?" went the subject line. The text of the message read simply, "Call if you need anything, -N." Below that was a forwarded link to an article in a local newsletter which masqueraded as a newspaper and was run by a notorious peddler of government conspiracies: "Horned Toddler Found Living Outside of Fairfield. Sources Suspect Drugs, the Occult." There under the headline was a candid photograph of little Jamie riding his tricycle in front of Helga. His hair was parted by the breeze of his forward motion on their way to the park, and there it was. He couldn't wear a helmet because of the growth, and she could just barely decipher it germinating up out of his forehead in the photograph. She recognized their clothes from Tuesday of the previous week but couldn't recall anyone taking their picture. Still, with everyone walking around with their phones out in front of them these days, she realized that it could've been anyone.

She didn't read the article. She didn't need to; the headline said it all.

Helga told Jamie then that the park would have to wait. She turned on PBS for the boy and went about stuffing their suitcases and duffle bags with food, clothing, and essential belongings—medicines, toiletries, passports. The grating voice of Caillou whined from the TV in the living room as Helga emptied their closets.

"Mama, why Caillou has no hair?" Jamie had asked once early into his time watching the cartoon show chronicling the exploits of a four-year-old Canadian boy. Helga looked it up for him and learned that the show's creators couldn't decide what kind of hair he should have and had somehow come to the conclusion that making him bald would appeal more universally to all children. This, despite the fact that he was obviously both a boy-child and white, and that baldness was perhaps the least common hairstyle of children anywhere.

"He was just born special without hair," Helga finally told Jamie, "like you and your pointer. Some people are born missing things; some people have extra." Jamie had accepted this explanation just fine.

When Helga finished gathering their most crucial items, she told Jamie she'd be out packing the car and would be back in just a minute. When she'd climbed the stairs again after the first load, however, the door to the apartment was ajar. She had only been gone a minute, no more than two.

She flung open the door only to be grabbed from behind by a man who covered her mouth with a gloved hand and immobilized her in some kind of excruciating hold. Another man was duct taping Jamie to a kitchen chair. The boy's mouth had already been taped shut and he looked up at his mother with furious eyes, though the precise mixture of fear and anger made him seem preternaturally more concerned with his mother's circumstances than his own. There had always been a temerity to the child that had unnerved her, and never before had she been more aware of this trait than in his expression right then.

"We won't hurt him, but if you scream we break both your necks," said the man holding her from behind, whom she still couldn't see. The accent was difficult to place, something Slavic maybe. He'd bent her arm back in such a way that she'd have to snap it in two in order to move.

The other man finished taping the child to the chair, and it was then she saw the hacksaw on the kitchen table. An unnatural moan bellowed up from her gut and could be felt throughout the room despite being muffled by the man with the gloved hands.

"We're not gonna hurt him; there's no nerve endings in bone. But this will do for us much more than it's doing for you. Do you know how much the horn of a baby rhino goes for on the black market? More than diamonds. More than gold."

She watched as the shadows of tree branches seemed to grasp at the man from the wall behind him, but the image soon blurred with her tears into a visual soup. The boy made no sound as the man lifted the hacksaw to his forehead, though Helga remembered feeling herself involuntarily regurgitate her morning oatmeal into the hand of the gloved man just before everything went black.

* * *

Helga could open her eyes before she could move, and for a few terrified moments she thought that Jamie was gone. She awoke expecting to see Jamie on the floor with blood trailing down his face, but there was only the puddle of her own breakfast blooming out from under her head. Then she saw him scamper around the corner from the bathroom with a towel, and all her breath and life returned to her at the same time.

"Mama, I help! You're sick." He handed her the towel, which she accepted and self-consciously used to wipe herself down as sobs overtook her in shuddering waves. She took Jamie in her arms and checked him over the way she'd done when he was just born. A few raised bands of red marked his arms and face from the duct tape, but that appeared to be all.

"Did you get out of the chair all by yourself?" she asked, incredulous. When she was a child, Helga wouldn't have even ripped off her own Band-aids; she'd have waited weeks until it was all gummed up and grimy, hanging by a few gooey threads, to peel it off gingerly under water in the bath.

Jamie nodded. She swept away the hair on his forehead to find that the nub of his protruding bone, formerly the length of a grown person's thumb, was now shorn flat into a jagged stump.

"Oh, baby," she said, obscuring most of her face with the towel to hide her reaction.

"It's okay. Okay? Don't cry." He touched his forehead and sighed, "Oh."

It occurred to Helga that they should leave right then. She felt an immediate and overwhelming impulse for them to completely disappear.

"Those were bad men. We're gonna go someplace nice where there's no bad men, okay? Someplace pretty and safe."

Helga changed her soiled shirt and dressed Jamie in his warmest fleece sweater.

"Let's go down to the marina and feed the ducks and drink hot cocoa with all the marshmallows you can eat." She boiled water for instant cocoa which she poured into a thermos and grabbed two mugs, extra sugar, and the entire remaining bag of marshmallows for the road.

They could walk to the marina from the apartment, so she carried down their red wagon to the sidewalk under one arm as she held Jamie's hand. The thermos of cocoa and other provisions knocked around on her back in a knapsack. She donned a wide-brimmed hat and sunglasses and made Jamie wear a sunhat as well. The autumn sun hovered low in the sky and seemed to aim directly into their eyes despite the hats and no matter which way they turned.

Helga made a point of changing direction to avoid crossing paths with other people on the street, so it was a twenty-minute walk to the water's edge. There, they reclined on a blanket from the wagon and proceeded to feed the ducks an entire loaf of marbled rye bread.

When the bread was gone and the ducks lost interest, Helga poured Jamie his mug of hot cocoa with two heaping spoonfuls of extra sugar and a fistful of marshmallows. They gulped their cocoa down as the sun dipped down toward the coastal mountain ridges to the west. When Jamie was full, she drank the rest of his as well.

"Let's go ride out on the water," she said. The boy quietly regarded the slough, which rippled in the late afternoon breeze and lit up like the scales of a fish. The whole serpentine waterway gleamed as one throbbing, pulsating beast.

"We'll grab us a rowboat and get going." He nodded in agreement at the idea, too young to comprehend that one generally needed to rent or own a rowboat in order to take one out, so the fact that they merely walked down to the water and unmoored one from the dock was unremarkable to the child. For all he knew, a dinghy was a public resource, as available to everyone as your average drinking fountain or city bikeshare.

"I'm hot," Jamie announced as Helga lifted him into the boat. "I'm sleepy."

"I know, buddy, I'm tired too," Helga replied. "It'll cool off once we get to the bay."

They abandoned the wagon and the still-spread blanket by the marina, and the two items together seemed to Helga to be waiting for something, perched there side-by-side at the edge of the marsh, as though some kids had merely dashed off to play a game of Frisbee and would soon return. The wagon in particular seemed watchful, its handle taut and tilted up like the rifle of a sentry.

"I'm sleepy," the boy said once again.

"Let's hunt for shorebirds," Helga suggested, already rowing in a rhythm down Suisun Slough away from town in the direction of Grizzly Bay. Tule reeds bordered the marsh and fingered up to the sky en masse reaching well above their heads, which made it so they could only see what was directly in front or behind them.

"Geese—honk-honk." Jamie pointed to several of them swimming behind the boat.

"There goes a coot!" cried Helga.

Jamie yawned. "Seagulls." Along with ducks, this was the limit of shorebirds that he could identify by name.

"Shall we count them?" He nodded ponderously.

"1," "1,"

A pelican swoops in beside them for an aquatic landing. Blue dragonflies stalk mosquitoes just above the surface.

"2," "2,"

An egret probes regally among the cattails. The sun sinks below the ridgeline, bleeding out a voltaic orange.

"3," "3,"

Over on a sandbar, a tawny killdeer scampers for bugs.

"4," "."

A common kestrel hoists a vole overhead, navigating back to her young.

"5," "."

A double-crested cormorant devours the hatchling of a snapping turtle as the rowboat coasts into the mouth of the bay.

"." "."

A pair of great blue herons soars in tandem, beaks lanced forward into the wind, heads held high, wings blazing.

MARLÉNE ZADIG is a lifelong Californian currently based in Berkeley with an MFA in Creative Writing from the University of Maryland. Her stories have recently appeared or are forthcoming in *Michigan Quarterly Review, StoryQuarterly, Bennington Review, Joyland, Cimarron Review, Necessary Fiction*, and elsewhere. Her work made Longform's top 5 list for Best of 2015 in Fiction, and she's been a runner-up for the 2017 Literary Awards at *The Pinch*, the 2016 *StoryQuarterly* Fiction Prize, the 2015 Fulton Prize for Short Fiction, and a winner of *Carve Magazine*'s First Annual Blog Contest. Her story collection manuscript, *Everybody Dies*, was recently named a finalist for the 2018 New American Fiction Prize, and she's now finishing up a novel about wildfire in the West.

KIM GARCIA

Homelands

Strolling the Bardo, flaneur, wishing into windows
where I am reflected. Plate glass, what an invention!
Walls of molten sand yielding view. The rain falling
on the just and the unjust. Sun also rising. A breath.

                                                Beloved,

move in closer. This plumb line we're orbiting
is a dark matter we can't stop talking about, probing
yes, yes, yes until we pass through customs, come
into the country where we are strangers at last.

KIM GARCIA is the author of *The Brighter House*, winner of the 2015 White Pine Press Poetry Prize, *DRONE*, winner of the 2015 Backwaters Prize, and *Madonna Magdalene*, released by Turning Point Books in 2006. Her poems have appeared in such journals as *Crab Orchard Review*, *Crazyhorse*, *Mississippi Review*, *Nimrod*, and *Subtropics*, and her work has been featured on The Writer's Almanac. Recipient of the 2014 Lynda Hull Memorial Prize, an AWP Intro

Writing Award, a Hambidge Fellowship, and an Oregon Individual Artist Grant, Garcia teaches creative writing at Boston College.

M.C. ARMSTRONG

Wapakoneta

I can still hear Wapakoneta that September evening we came riding under the face of the moon against a corn silk wind.
"Listen," I said, pulling up next to Jonah and Sky Hoof.
In twenty years, the village would be gone. But that night, caught in the air were the sounds of families, laughter and dogs, drums and pots, ocarinas and chants, the prayers of old men rising up like smoke to that face in the moon, and like many of the men down there in the village, I wanted to believe that the Spirit had returned to us and that, just like the seeds in the spring soil, we were all about to be reborn.
As we rode into camp, I heard the sound of a bottle breaking against a tree. And then another. We followed the split-rail fence until the fence opened through a latch and a black dog leapt out and started barking at our heels. That dog followed us for a piece as we passed the smoking cottages of my elders, the gaunt and smiling faces of my past. I could see my father's home on the far side of the village beyond the sawmill and the gristmill and the acres of corn. I could see the melons and pumpkins like the severed heads of war returning peacefully to the earth and I could hear the wet clicking of the hogs in their mud. My wife's sister and her kids came running up to us as we dismounted our horses outside the council house where I noticed a

white trader talking to one of our people, a short rat-faced man I'd never seen before.

"If you don't want it, that's fine, but you can't just destroy it and not pay for it," the trader said.

The rat-faced man threw a curse at the white man. We were busy hugging and telling our stories to my wife's sister and her children, and a good part of my mind wanted nothing more than to ride a little longer to my father and just bed down for the night after dinner. But there was something wild in the eye of that young rat-faced man and something terrified in the face of that trader, and I could see the shards of brown glass all over the ground and could smell the sweet stink of the liquor in the dirt.

"My god, Jonah. Is that you?" said the trader.

"McKee," Jonah said.

Jonah was my friend. He was the one who had returned to me my daughter from the American traitor, St. Clair, and he was traveling with me because he wanted the bounty as much as I wanted the scalp. Jonah shook hands with the white man and I felt warm listening to them talk about the war and the weather and how it was always so much more interesting here in our village than down south at the place they called Fort Amanda.

"So you wanted to get away from the old coop?" Jonah said.

"I bring a case of whiskey," McKee said, "because I pay my debts and that was how they wanted them paid. I offered meat, but they asked for whiskey. They're the ones who asked."

"You came alone?" Jonah asked.

McKee nodded. Which was a testament to the peaceful spirit of our people. There was a war raging up along the map lines to the northwest and there was a military supply fort—Fort Amanda—just twenty miles away from us to the south, but that white man, McKee, rode his horse on his own to visit my people and that is the truth to remember.

"Where you headed?" McKee asked, walking alongside us.

"North," Jonah said with a smile.

McKee understood that smile in the same way I understood the way my wife's sister ran her tongue under her lower lip. I knew that look real good. That tongue was saying the exact opposite of what McKee's smile said. Men and women have different minds when it comes to war.

"Redding lost an arm back in April," McKee said. "Darrow's dead."

"We ran into a man who told us we nearly lost Fort Stephenson," Jonah said.

"But we didn't," McKee said.

I studied the face of McKee. I've seen millions like him and suspect I'll see a few more before I die. Some men talk about death with a warrior shine in their eye that tells you they know there are things on this earth far scarier than losing your life. It's like they, too, know the great secret that none of us will ever die.

"Sheekeetha!"

My father called out to my brother first. I left Jonah and McKee to talk about war and I ran to my mother who was hugging Little Moon, my daughter, and thanking The Great Spirit for returning her granddaughter.

"Hahkawisalawsimama," my mother said, asking my daughter if her spirit was still with us. And I felt my daughter nodding her head into my mother's breasts the way I must have when I was feeding as a baby. My relatives came running out of their cottages and wigwams to greet us, and soon enough I was back in my father's house hearing all the stories I'd missed about the hunts and the harvests, the new babies and the new drunks, my father taking us all inside the house to pour whiskey for the men. I watched him greedily sniff the mouth of the bottle. On the table I noticed a calfskin bible.

"Here," he said.

I held my cup like intended to drink. I beheld my father in his European shirt and his silver necklace studded with red trade beads, a brown blanket belted around his waist above his breech-cloth, his belly poking out like my daughter wasn't the only one pregnant. He wore new buckskin leggings and new moccasins and I wondered how much he'd traded for his beads and cotton and if maybe the traders had thrown the bible in for free as they sometimes did.

I pretended to drink from my cup. The smell alone made me

wild. It felt good to be home, to see my daughter safe again in her grandmother's arms. Women can be funny. My mother was undoing my wife, Koku's, braids from the night before as Koku tried to talk to my cousins, but I could see Koku eyeing my mom the way a dog will watch another dog eating out of its dish. Meanwhile, Sheekeetha drank down a second glass of my father's whiskey and was telling everyone about how I was going to bring war to the doors of every house in the village by doing what I was about to do to that man named St. Clair.

"Little Angry finally got angry and the white man's now selling him on joining the Big Knives," Sheekeetha said.

"That's a lie," I said.

"You're not angry that your daughter is pregnant with a white man's child?"

"You speak like they do when you drink whiskey," I said.

"Is it a lie?"

I took a good long smell from that clay cup. My eyes angled toward that calfskin bible. I looked at my father and his cloudy wizened eyes. Seven years earlier he had visited Thomas Jefferson in the White House. He was one of only a dozen men in our village who could both speak and read the white man's tongue. I felt I could speak my brother's snake mind if I drank that devil's drink my father had given me and I also felt that maybe it would be good to release the demons, as the white men often say. Maybe sons and fathers, after a long time apart, need to do what is necessary to bring the spirit into the room.

"You tell the half truths," I said to my brother.

"What part is a lie?" Sheekeetha said.

Talk makes fools out of men. I wanted to tell Sheekeetha and everyone in that room that what brings war to homes is the same thing that brings babes into the world. I wanted to throw my cup across the room and tell them all about how The Prophet was right. Some have already forgotten him, but there was once a Kispoko who lived among us and built a village beyond our village in a town called Greenville. Some called him Lalawethika. Some called him Tenskwatawa. This prophet was given visions by the very spirits that took our visions away and these visions showed him our people in a dark hot realm drinking endless cups of liquid lead, the white man's whiskey turned to the very hot river of rock that forges the guns and bullets we all still use to kill each other. The prophet saw it all as one—the whiskey, the bullet, and the gun. And so he ceased drinking the liquid bullets and built his village and just as he saw the metals and the rums as one, he knew that all people were one, and so he invited the Delaware and the Wyandot and the Potawotami and anyone else who shared his vision to listen to his prophecies, and I journeyed to that village by myself one summer. I met The Prophet and his brother, Tecumseh. I heard his words. I sat at his feet by the council fire and tore off the trade beads I wore around my neck. I promised The Prophet I would never stop hunting and would never surrender to the spirits that were dividing our people. I embraced him under a moon like a fisherman's hook and he whispered into my ear:

"Your father was a good man," he said. "But he is no longer a man."

I never returned to Greenville after that night. But I wanted to use The Prophet's words to fight back my brother's lies. I wanted everyone in my father's house to feel how foolish words can make us when you divide them up the way we'd been dividing the Kispoko and the Maykujay, the Miami and the Delaware.

"Have more," I said, dumping my cup into Sheekeetha's.

And it was only then, as I burst out the door and stormed up to the edge of the corn the white men mash into whiskey that I realized I hadn't seen Jonah or McKee inside my father's house. I stood there under the tossed kernels of stars and stared at the tassels and the stalks and listened to the crickets and the drums, and even though I wasn't drunk, I swayed in the wind like the maize and I called out for my friend. I saw his sawbones tied up next to my mustang, his binoculars hanging off his saddle. And I walked back into my father's house to make sure my eyes hadn't been playing tricks on me. But there were no white men in my father's house. And outside, in the night, it was just the lines of corn standing and swaying like some kind of army beneath the stars, like the war was already right outside my father's door.

I looked up at the sky and saw an arrowhead falling apart, like it was shedding feathers. I felt it all coming. And I was afraid. A part of me wanted to walk back inside my father's house and call for the bottle, let that spirit wash back my confusion. It was strange to be home and feel so far away. I walked over to Jonah's horse.

"Hello, Patrick," I said.

I could tell Wolf, my horse, was getting jealous, sniffing and stomping at the way I was whispering and petting on Patrick. I heard an owl not too far away, an old man singing and changing his song at that exact moment to ape the call of the owl, and I decided to follow the song, to take a walk through the village. I didn't want to go back inside and pretend everything was okay with my father. And it was funny the way my son walked out of my house just as I was walking away. It was like he was feeling me the same way that old man was feeling that owl, and when he asked me what I was doing outside, I told him to just look around and listen. When I could tell he wasn't satisfied with that explanation, I told him half of the truth. I told him I was worried about Jonah.

"I saw them," he said. "They went off with that man we saw when we arrived."

"What man?"

"The one with the teeth."

"The one that looked like a rat?"

Sky Hoof nodded. I looked up at that arrowhead cloud. Its point was all gone.

"I want to go with you to Canada," he said.

"You can't," I said. "I need you to stay here and watch over your sister. She needs you."

"I want to kill the man that put the devil in her," he said.

"She doesn't have the devil in her," I said.

"She says she does," he said.

"Come on," I said. "Let's go for a walk."

It hurt me to think about my daughter. We skirted the corn. I kept looking through the vents in the rows, like I might find Jonah there on his back, looking up at the stars, singing a song. But the feeling I had was getting worse and it was not only because I didn't know or trust that rat-faced man I'd seen breaking the bottles, but it was also on account of having to hide the truth from my son. I didn't want him worrying about my journey north. I was glad when our silence was broken by the old man.

He had milkstone eyes like I do now. He was singing his songs in front of Black Hoof's house, a young girl studying the chants at his feet and staring at the glowing wafers of wood burning in the fire, a doll in her hands. I knew the old man. He was the brother of the one we called Waweyapersenwaw. Blue Jacket. I could tell you a million tales about the worlds that man had seen before he stopped seeing. His name was Flying Jack. He jumped atop a deer and cut its throat and rode its dying body down the Hocking Hills. He could run as fast as a mustang and some say faster. My grandfather told me that Flying Jack once put an arrow straight through the ear of an American from a thousand feet away and then licked the fletching on a second arrow and put another in the opposite ear as that man was twisting down to the earth in his final death dance. As Sky Hoof and I stood over his fire, I asked Flying Jack about the state of the Spirit.

"Little Angry," he said, remembering me just from my voice, some faint thread of song still carrying on in his throat, a wheezy moan not entirely unlike the shrill hiss a wet log makes when the fire starts to scare out the water.

"The Spirit is strong," he said. "Maybe too strong tonight."

"What do you mean too strong?"

A silence fell. The old man now lived in a wigwam next to old Black Hoof's house. I wondered if the girl with the doll was his granddaughter and if her mother and father were near. I looked for light behind Black Hoof's door. He was our Chief and he was a good man.

"I heard you calling the white man's name," Flying Jack said.

"You heard right," I said.

"Jonah! Jonah! Jonah!"

Flying Jack changed his voice. I'd never heard my voice so high like a child's. I tried to smile away my fear so my son wouldn't see it, but there was no fooling Sky Hoof. He could feel what the old man was feeling. He and the little girl with the red-faced doll that was made out of the white man's sacking both stared into Flying Jack's cobweb eyes.

"I hear that name all the time," Flying Jack said. "The Christians who come here to cut our hair and give us pigs—they talk about this Jonah. They say he got swallowed up by a big fish and lived in the belly of that beast beneath the faces of those seas we've never seen. Well, they are right about one thing. We are all like that man, Little Angry. Waiting to be released. Waiting in the dark. Waiting to be coughed up onto a bright beach where we might see again. But tonight I am afraid because I hear you calling that name and I hear our people all day calling another name and the names are all different, Little Angry. But it is all the same cry. All the same prayer."

He closed his eyes and drummed his lids like he might grace his eyes with the vision of youth if he struck the right beat. He opened them again real wide and smiled.

"Jonah is my friend," I said.

"And Tecumseh was once mine," he said.

"Tecumseh?" Sky Hoof said.

Even now, that name still lives like lightning on the tongues of my people. Maybe it still echoes in you, faint as the hiss of an ember before it turns back to earth.

"He is our final eye," Flying Jack said. "Black Hoof has accepted the whiteness, the blindness. Blue Jacket is dead. Your grandfather is dead. And now your father is like the others. He accepts the pigs and the beads and the Christian stories that tell men to stop being men. But tonight, Tecumseh still fights, so tonight the Spirit is still strong."

"Is he here?" Sky Hoof asked.

"He is out there, where he will always be. Where we will always be," Flying Jack responded.

I could see the gleam in my son's eye, that warrior worship I myself fell prey to from time to time. But there is a difference between the eyes of a son, the eyes of a father, and the milk-stoned eyes of an old man.

"They will kill us all if we fight with Tecumseh," I said.

"They will kill us all if we don't," Flying Jack said.

My son looked to me for an answer and so did the little girl who fingered the blood red braid of that doll. I looked into the throbbing coals of the fire, the smooth oak log now scaled like the sloughed skin of a snake, like you could see its orange heart beating beneath its black skin.

"There is another path," I said.

"Speak of it," said Flying Jack.

"You heard the owl earlier. Just as we were walking your way," I said. "I heard her call out and I heard you call back in the same way you mocked me calling out for my friend."

Flying Jack nodded and smiled. Even if someone is about to disagree with you, I suppose it feels good to know that at least they're listening, especially when ears are all you've got left. I looked into my son's eyes as I tried to describe the path I wanted him to take.

"We need to be like the owl," I said. "Not like the pig. Not like the sheep. Not like the geese. We cannot live our lives if we move in the fold and the flock. They tell us to fight with them, the reds and the blues. They tell us if we do, we can stay here in Wapakoneta, but it is all the same like you say. They want us where they can get us, grandfather. All of us together, so easy to trim and slaughter. Wear the red. Wear the blue. Stay inside the split-rail fence. Wapakoneta, Washington, Greenville—it is all the same, grandfather. We need to learn from the owl. We all know the owl is out there, where the Spirit is. But no one ever eats the owl because the owl is smart. She only calls out from time to time. When an owl spreads her wings and flies down out of the sky, everyone knows they are seeing the flash of the Spirit, the way. That is the path. That, my son, is why you cannot travel with Jonah and me into the north."

"The Jonah you call out for like an owl?"

Flying Jack gave me the Flying Jack face, his tongue out like a wolf. I almost conceded the point. Maybe if my son hadn't been listening, I would've given the old man that final ground. But my pride was hurt and my son was listening and so was that little girl, her eyes still unskinned by the cruelties of the world, the way the seasons and the treaties and even the words of your own brothers beat you back.

"I didn't call out for him like an owl," I said. "I called out for him like a man, like a friend. There is a difference."

"Hmmm," Flying Jack said. "Good luck with your difference."

That was when my son asked the old man to tell him more about the warrior we called Tecumseh.

"Hoooo," Flying Jack said, like an owl. "Hooo hooo! Listen."

And my son listened.

And so did I.

"Hssssssssssss," hissed Flying Jack.

But not like a snake.

The little girl smiled and pulled her doll against her heart.

"You can hear the panther on the wind," Flying Jack said. "Listen."

The wind rose and, like an echo from the hissing song in the fire, it seethed like a cat when you crawl up on its den. The old man told us how Tecumseh—whose name means panther in the sky—came from the Kispoko, the panther people and how his father, Pukshinwah, a Creek, married his mother, Meethotaaske, a Shawnee.

"His mother was a turtle," Flying Jack said. "When you cross the wisdom of the turtle with the speed of the panther, you breed the wind of the warrior into the child's spirit. But not every child crossed with panther and turtle becomes a Tecumseh. He was one of eight kids. When he was younger than you, he saw his papa killed by the white man. He was never the same, child. Death changes people."

Flying Jack gave us the Flying Jack face, but his tongue didn't hang so long when he said what he said about death. His milkstone eyes flickered with flame. The wind turned and curled under the logs like Tecumseh was with us, just as I am with you. Stories are funny that way, the way they bring back the dead. The old man put his chin on his crossed hands.

"Fathers give sons brothers in case the fathers join the spirits too soon," Flying Jack said. "Tecumseh was raised by Cheeseekah, his oldest brother. His younger brother, the prophet, was a triplet, another sign from Moneto, just like the earthquake and the star shot from last year, the way the spirit finally rubbed his thumb across the night. One of the last things I saw before I lost my sight. Maybe that trail of light was the thing that blinded me."

I, too, had seen what the white men called the comet seven seasons ago. I, too, had felt the earthquake, that day when the land moved like the white men were nothing more than plates and cups the Spirit could clear away by tilting her table.

"Tenskwatawa, Tecumseh's wisest brother, was more turtle and Tecumseh more panther, but together," Flying Jack said, "they embodied the strongest force a Shawnee ever feels: brotherhood. Tecumseh couldn't stay married to his wife, Mamate. Most men feel what Tecumseh felt. They don't want to just stay home and read the Bible and feed pigs. They want to fight for the Spirit, for the earth. But they don't have a brother to watch the moon while they watch the sun. Without eyes in your back, you'll always be like a turtle without a shell or a cat without claws. But Tecumseh had Tenskwatawa and they built the city in the west for Moneto and the people from all the tribes all came together and even the few whites who wear the beards and want peace came to the place they called Prophetstown and they prayed together with the panther and the turtle. Thousands came. They moved like the birds are moving right now, like they could feel the heat of the Spirit's fire. They flocked and gathered and listened. They listened."

Just as we all listened to the wind and the hiss of the fire, the drunk noises of the village. Flying Jack could hear those loud drunk voices. You could see it in his face, the sadness. He knew he was dying alongside the ears of his people. But not on account of the bottle.

"Your own chief—the man who sleeps in this house behind me," he said, "has told me on a number of occasions, that he, too, took the pilgrimage west to the feet of the Prophet and that he would've stayed there, but his legs are bad and his eyes almost as gone as mine and so his warring days are done and how can a chief tell his people to go to war if he himself can no longer fight?"

The old man knew what he was doing talking about Black Hoof like that, raising his voice with the rising wind. Sure enough, the old chief with his stiff legs walked out of his house with his hair wild and gray and his ears flopping with silver and glass, scars all over his chest.

"You're no good," he said to Flying Jack, which made the old man smile.

My chief wrapped me in his warm arms and gathered my son in, too. He left his door half open, but I saw the fingers of one of his wives or daughters reach out and close that door. Maybe they didn't want to hear the men talk more about war, but that little girl with the doll sure did. She had her hand up under that doll's dress like she was going to use her fingers to make that thing talk sure as I'm about to do the same to my old chief.

"Why are you out here telling lies?" Black Hoof said.

"That's what words do," Flying Jack said.

I wish I could freeze that fiery moment in ice: my son in my arms, my chief smiling like a fox, the village of my people more than just puppets and ghosts, words on a page. Real—that's the English word for it. It was all still real in that moment. When I heard a cry down the path, I thought at first it was that arched back cry that a woman makes to tell the world the tribe will live on. Black Hoof's face turned serious.

"Why don't you tell the boy about what Tecumseh said to General Harrison before they killed his brother? Why don't you tell him what his brother said about how we'll never die just before he was killed?"

The old man slouched like a doll that had just lost the interest of the child, the hand no longer holding up the back.

"Tenskwatawa was right," Flying Jack said. "We will never die if we do what the Spirit asks. But we didn't do it and we never have."

"What did Tenskwatawa want us to do?" my son asked with his eyes as fine and combed with gold and jade as the old man's were with milk and web.

"He said we must all fight as one for all who see all as one. He walked right up to General Harrison's white palace and stood in front of that man who bribed all our drunks into selling away the land of all of our warriors and he thundered at the American General. He said to him and all the drunk slaves the General has made with pigs and beads and rum and fear of the land of the dead, "How do you do it, Harrison? How do you sell a country? What is this word, country?

Why not sell the air, the sea, and the entire earth?" After he said that, the white people laughed at Tecumseh until they turned red and then they got drunk to pretend that they never saw the red and they woke up and they twisted Tecumseh's words around in their newspapers so they could get more drunks to sign more treaties. And then they marched in with their guns and their torches into the Prophet's home and they killed the women and the children the same way they kill the black man. To teach a lesson, as they say. They burned the entire village to the ground to teach us another lesson."

I had heard this story before, but never with my son close. Every day an old man crawls into the mind of a child with words about war. I didn't want my son going to war. But I could feel what he was feeling by the fire. He was feeling the fire. And then we both heard that wild cry again, and we both knew there was no man left in Wapakoneta with enough panther in his blood to make a woman scream like that. That was no woman screaming beyond the corn. And it was no Shawnee, either.

We ran along the cornstalks until I could see what I already knew was coming. That was when I grabbed Sky Hoof and told him to run back and get his uncle. When my son said no I slapped him in the face so hard it dropped him to his knees. I'll never forget the angry way he looked into the corn while he was down on the ground, like if he concentrated a little harder he could turn into a snake and slither down the rows.

"Go!" I said.

I watched my son give up on being a snake and do what he was told, running back the way we'd come past Black Hoof who was walking as fast as an old man can, Flying Jack still back there by the fire with his milkstone eyes and the little girl and her doll, the old man probably weaving my son's running right into the end of his story.

I could see the spirit shadows in the grass. I could see the half-circle of my brothers around the playground behind the house of one of Black Hoof's nephews, a man named Red Lake. A big patch of cleared away earth where the kids played war shone like a seared scar where the comet landed, the fire down there by that crowd ten times bigger than Flying Jack's and there were no children with dolls and there was nobody sitting. They were all standing and dancing and they had Jonah and McKee tied up to the same big oak tree, their faces painted black, both men totally naked, McKee bleeding from his chest.

    I have seen the fear of death on men's faces before. But I'd never in my life seen anything like I saw in the eyes of that trader, McKee, an arrow already in his side, his white eyes wishing they were comets that could leap out of their sockets and away from what was coming. McKee saw it all, or as much as the eyes of men can see before they close. Yes, I believe he saw what I saw: a sky of helpless stars looking down like old milkstone eyes on the rat-faced man laughing like crazy while a smaller fellow I'd never seen before with a single eagle feather banded around his forehead was screaming a curse in a tongue even I didn't fully understand. To this day, I do not know how far away that man with the eagle feather flew to be in Wapakoneta that night. I wonder if he came from the lands they now call California. Did he, like the Prophet, see distant shores where the white men walked the red men into the seas of burning lead, making them drink like horses until they can't drink whiskey no more, only to keep them drinking? What had that strange man with the eagle feather seen that had filled him with such hate and wild?

    "Stop!" I called out.

    But when the man with the eagle feather caught my eye in the firelight, he didn't turn into a snake and slither away. He just smiled. The rat-faced man stood up straight from his laughing coil and his eyes followed bashfully down the path to where Black Hoof ambled. Everyone in that half-circle turned away from the tree where the two white men were tied the way our coastal ancestors tied themselves when the hurricanes came. Everyone seemed willing to wait to hear what we had to say before letting the killing of those white men go on. Everyone but the one with the eagle feather.

    "Hsssssss!" he screamed at me, like he had heard Flying Jack's story and now aimed to live the purpose of the panther.

    Spirit, I don't know why you do what you do.

What a wild cry that stranger released as he tossed his tomahawk toward the tree. And that hawk found its mark just like a cormorant diving down for a fish. My people went quiet. I heard the sound of McKee's life going out of his body as quiet as the skitter of a squirrel up a tree. McKee's body then did the dance death makes you do when you're not quite ready to give up the shirt of your skin. Like a child shaking her fingers out of a puppet's cloth. No sooner was that dance done than that man with the eagle feather had his knees on McKee's back, his scalping knife moving in a sharp tight circle around his head, and there was a sudden slit in that killer's eyes as he cut into McKee while staring straight at Jonah.

"Good," I heard one man say.

"This will be bad for us," said another.

My village was divided by fear. We were like your North and South. Your Adam and Eve. We ate the fruit with you. We could see you, and so we could no longer see. But some of us believed we could. That man with the eagle feather was not afraid of me or Black Hoof or the dozen turned heads who were waiting for their chief to either praise or condemn the killing of the whites.

"Hello," said that wild-eyed stranger in English, holding his knife in front of Jonah's face.

That man with the eagle feather was not afraid of Jonah, but he did seem suddenly interested in him, like he wanted to study Jonah just a little bit longer than McKee. That cat-slit I saw in his eyes was like a mirror of what I saw in Jonah. Like it was the first time in the stranger's life he'd seen a white man prepared to die and like he wanted to savor it like a pipe of strong smoke in the winter at the top of a mountain.

"You're going to get us all killed!" I yelled as I ran toward the tree with my tomahawk drawn. I slipped into that hot hissing space between Jonah and the man with the eagle feather. I put my palm against Jonah's head and the blade of my tomahawk a hair away from the nose of the stranger. I turned toward my people and put my foot atop the bloodied ribs of McKee.

"We will all die for this," I said. "This dead man is from Fort Amanda."

"We should burn Fort Amanda!" replied one of my people.

"Like they burned Prophetstown!" cried another.

"So we become like them and burn the whole earth?" I said.

And then, just before the stranger spoke to me in my own tongue, he ran the dripping underside of McKee's hairy scalp down my tomahawk blade like some kind of lewd act, like some kind of christening, as the white men say. Like he knew he could say something with that hairy flesh slicking my axe that no man can ever say with words.

"You," he said.

I said nothing to that.

"You like them," he said.

He smiled with those same cat-slit eyes, like he was trying to hide that white skin we all possess. I could feel Jonah throbbing behind me, his body at war with his face. We're always at war.

"This man is my brother," I said.

"I am your brother," the stranger said.

"I have never met you," I said.

"I have met you," he said.

"Where? When?" I said.

"Every day," he said. "Everywhere I go I see you sign the treaties. I see you take big laughing drinks from the white man's whiskey. You have had whiskey with this one, haven't you?"

I wish I could say that I maintained the same wildcat scowl as that man and Jonah. But I looked away toward the rat-faced man and all the eyes of my people and I could see a white woman that one of my cousins had married walking up on the scene and I could see Black Hoof looking older and weaker than he'd ever looked before, like he could see the next war coming and the next one after that and all of us getting marched out of Wapakoneta and into the blood of the western sun. I looked down at the scar of the earth where all the grass had been kicked away by the play of children and I saw a single silver bead in that soil, like a tear from the moon. But rather than lie to my people and tell them I'd never taken a drink with Jonah, I jumped like a panther out of its den and split that stranger in half with my tomahawk, and I took his eagle feather and planted it in the split and I took his blood and used it to redden the black on Jonah's face and I cut Jonah free with the very scalping knife that man had used on

McKee and we walked for a moment with our faces painted in the same blood of that stranger as I said to my people:

"This man is my brother. This man is your brother. He saved my daughter. He saved your sister. And you stand and laugh and paint him black like none of you has ever taken a drink of the whiskey or received a kindness from an American."

I held my tomahawk up to the moon to dip it into that great egg of light. I looked my people in the eye and ran the blade around the crescent of their faces, their fearful frozen bodies. I knew all of them by name. Red Lake. Big George. Little Horse. I knew them all. I knew the ones who liked whiskey and I knew the ones who had broken bread with the Quakers and the ones who had planted their seeds in the white man's women. But I also knew the ones who, like Tecumseh, had seen their fathers and mothers murdered by the whites, the ones who had seen their brothers go crazy on the laughing waters, their sisters tied to trees and defiled in the same way they'd done to Jonah and McKee and my daughter. So just as I was realizing how no words could end the war—I returned to what I'd said in the beginning.

"This man is my brother," I said.

And then we ran for our horses.

M.C. ARMSTRONG's fiction and essays have appeared in *Esquire*, *The Mantle*, *The Missouri Review*, *The Gettysburg Review*, *Mayday*, *Monkeybicycle*, *Epiphany*, *The Literary Review*, and other journals and anthologies. In 2008 he embedded with Joint Special Operations Forces in Al Anbar Province, Iraq as a field reporter. Currently, he is a PhD candidate in Global War on Terror Studies at the University of North Carolina at Greensboro.

BIX GABRIEL

Once

O nce, a woman sat down to eat her lunch.

Josanna, or Josy, as her new friends called her, set the tiered lunch box – a recent purchase to accommodate single portions – on the table abutting the window. She spread the napkin across her lap, smoothing the square that was like a postcard on the billboard of her thighs. Not that she was advertising anything. But her new pants, black stretch velvet, announced herself as herself. Today, she was having the lunch she'd craved for weeks. She had dressed for the occasion.

From the top-most container of the mini-tower, chunks of beef studded with peppercorns glimmered up at her. Fried onions glistened in the ridges. She had cooked the dish that morning, in the kitchenette she shared with Lena, the electric burner as low as it could go so that the onion melted into the meat. Unlike every time she'd made it before, for the children, for Jochim, this time she ground the pepper mill six, seven, eight times, the powder collecting in clumps whose edges darkened in the fat.

Finally, she had the office to herself. After weeks of waiting, her colleagues were away, and her boss, Giulia, was out for lunch. Josanna unfastened the second tier in the tower. The parathas she'd wrapped in foil were still hot. From the small desk that barely contained her, Josanna's view was the basilica of Santa Maria di Collemaggio, its cracked blue dome the colour of the sky, so that the sky itself appeared broken. The Apennine Mountains spread like a watercolour beyond the limits of L'Aquila. If she looked down to the piazza, she'd see the children, six year olds who stomped in the water, teenagers who took pains to keep their bangs dry, couples lolling against the curve of the fountain, leaning into each other for a kiss every now and then. She wondered if A and D would be like that, scarcely looking away from their phones to nuzzle girls in public. Children, when she left them, now two years ago, she couldn't conjure them any differently, A's chubbiness at nine, D, though _a year younger, inching his way toward teenage.

She wiped down her plate, porcelain edged with blue, thirteen years old, as old as her marriage would have been. The plates were the only objects to travel with her – from India on that first and last journey to London, and now to Italy. They were one of the few items she'd chosen for her trousseau – her dowry, if she were being honest, though her Catholic parents liked to believe they were above the Hindu custom.

She felt something move behind her. Instantly, she spun around. Surveyed the room, twice, thrice. Nothing. But she sensed something or someone. She scolded herself, "Don't be a fool."

***

The day Josanna arrived in L'Aquila, the nuns made fresh pasta, rolling the dough over the wooden frame strung with wires, ribbons of fresh cannarozzetti falling like hair. Lena, obviously-dyed-red ponytail pulled tightly away her plump face, pushed over a plate of egg crepes. "Eat. You missed lunch."

Josanna loved the Italian way of drawing out the sounds of the last letter, "Eattt," misseduh," "lunchuh," "latehh." It made her less self-conscious about her own English, accented with the Malayalam that all the years of living in Croydon had not chiseled away. She took a cautious bite and snorted at the fieriness of the crepe.

"In L'Aquila, we havvuh, eh, we are famous for la diavolillo pepperoncino," said Lena. "How you likuhh?"

Josanna nodded, and Lena sat down with her at the table, easily taking up two seats, her girth wider than Josanna's, though that would change once they both enrolled in the 'Healthy Living' program that the shelter introduced the next month, after which the egg crepes were taken off the menu.

At mass that first evening, Josanna noticed Giulia, the only outsider to the shelter's residents. She saw her again at the monthly Circle of Prayer, nuns and laywomen praying and talking and eating together. Josanna's diffidence and lack of Italian prevented her from joining the group with the eagerness that gains approval and opens circles. But fat people are not meant to be shy. So everyone took Josanna for standoffish.

When Giulia said she was looking for a junior designer, but "someone who does not talk, talk, talk all day and night," Josanna submitted her application with the meager portfolio she had assembled during the graphic design classes that the shelter offered.

At the interview, Giulia, who headed the design and print division at the Studi Universitari Santa Maria di L'Aquila, asked, "Why did you come to Italy, to our little town here, Josy?"

Josanna had opened her mouth to say what she was thinking, that she'd seen L'Aquila on television, clips of the hills, the cobbled side streets, captured before the earthquake, and later as the rubble disintegrated, the nuns helping to clear the debris, and the ticker on the screen with the phone number of the convent taking in women and children who had become homeless. Somehow the number had stuck in her mind, though she had no consciousness of memorizing it, and it had come to her months later, after she'd heard from the last shelter she'd contacted in London, all of which were full.

She said, "I saw the news of the earthquake. I wanted to help." Giulia's severe glasses slipped down the bridge of her nose. The earthquake of 2009 had brought L'Aquila attention that not every resident appreciated. Though the church preached charity, pity was unwelcome.

Josanna added, "I needed — need, a home, for me, my children." It was the first time she'd mentioned the children, the idea of a new home, to anyone outside the shelter. But Giulia probably knew her story. Josanna felt the job slipping away. A moment later, Giulia smiled.

***

Josanna stole through the main office area, an open-floor plan dominated by a long worktable, where the designers looked at proofs through their loupes. The office was empty, the reason she had chosen today for the lunch she'd been craving. Fabiola, Susanna, and Enrico, the other designers, were at a conference in Rome, giddy at the big city. Ricardo, the art director, was in Paris celebrating some occasion with his boyfriend.

Josanna flipped the switch and the office flooded with light. She scrutinized the vacant desks, absorbing the hum of machines that had replaced silence. No sign of a single living thing.

It was impossible for anyone to enter the office without Josanna noticing. The old lift creaked and groaned and arrived at their floor with a jarring shudder that was unmistakable. She swung open Giulia's door. Empty.

Josanna returned to her own tiny office at the other end of the floor, telling herself that she was being paranoid, hearing sounds, imagining ghosts. She locked her room and stood just inside the door, seeing and re-seeing the space she had made her own.

The room had been a repository for everything that the University's design and production office had created until 1997, when the digital era crept in. Fifteen years later, the office still produced printed material but their storage now was a server, and a row of hard drives. When she first saw it, the old storage room was a jumble of placards advertising film screenings and performances of Teatro Di Pietra, magenta brochures with black type yellowed at the edges, a hundred versions of booklets for departments that no longer existed, and strewn among the paper, blocks of ampersands and typefaces. Josanna had the urge to pocket the most beautiful letters of the Bodoni font: A and D. Running her thumb against the ridges of the typeface, she'd felt the coarse stubble of A's shaven head the day after his first soccer match, a loss he'd borne silently, his body rigid in his bed when she said goodnight. The curve of the d was D's fist against her thigh when the lights went out in the Tube. In the end, she'd cleared out the room, organized the materials, and placed the typefaces in the windowsill, an open secret of her yearning.

Now, from against the door, Josanna's eyes searched shelf, bookcase, cabinet, rug, bin, canvas for an intruder. Another rustle came from the locked cupboard. She tiptoed over. Nothing to be seen. She placed her ear against the wood. She felt the wood beating, the forest's heart within the door. She pulled her chest away, her upper body, her shoulders an animal's: ear cocked, eye sharp, entire body alert. She caught herself re-living what had once been a daily habit, one that she was still unlearning a year after the practice was necessary.

***

On her second wedding anniversary, Josanna made a special meal. That evening she'd let the meat crisp, char, "just short of burned," the way Chef Sanjay Thomas recommended on TV. From the door, her lip between her teeth, she'd watched Jochim biting into a piece, seeming to savor it until he said, "What is this?"

Before she could explain, he continued, "Why do you have to watch me all the time? You think I'm the idiot in the idiot box?"
She'd returned to the kitchen and stayed there until she smelled his after-meal cigarette.

Over the next few days, she found little parcels of masticated beef deposited in nooks around the apartment: in the sleeve of her blouse, under a vase, among her jewelry; reaching for the light switch, her fingers had come away clammy from a fleshy gob tucked at the base of the lamp on her night-stand.

For months she lay awake questioning how she had misjudged Jochim so acutely, berating herself for her cooking, her experiments, her ineptitude, her expanding waist-line. When she became pregnant, she increased the fervor of her prayers. First out of self-pity, then from fear, then for forbearance. She gave up eating meat as a bargain with the Lord, safety in exchange for sacrifice. Now thirteen years later, the deal was done.

***

In the room that had been forgotten, that she'd made her own, Josanna's hand rose to her chest, her lungs tight. From a tube of posters, a shadow scurried out and scampered down the shelf. Josanna forced herself to breathe out a big gust of air. The grey-brown shape of a mouse surged up the leg of her desk. She shouted, "Ay, you dirty little rascal thing!"

The mouse sped up, racing faster than her eye could make out. "My lunch, oh, oh, oh!" She leapt towards her desk.

***

The day of her departure she'd invited Smiley, Jochim's cousin, for tea. Smiley lived in West Croydon, only twenty minutes away and for a while, the two families had made a tradition of Sunday lunch together. But since Smiley's husband Anthony had hurt his back working at the distillery, Smiley worked weekend shifts at Tesco's. Now, on a weekday, she'd been delighted to get away from Anthony and her own fifteen-year old, a boy-man who ordered his mother about like everyone else did.

Four o'clock, Josanna had said, and had kept her phone on until ten past, when she received the first confused message from Smiley, saying, "I'm outside your flat, chechi, where are you? I'm waiting." It was only after that voicemail that she'd destroyed the SIM card, knowing that Smiley would be at the door when D arrived from school in a few minutes, demanding food. She'd left them a feast: homemade pastries, bakery-bought cream puffs, cake, an assortment of biscuits. It was her one give-away, but one that everyone would assume was for Smiley's benefit. D would devour the mince curry puffs he loved but would A recognize his favorite, the round sweet-salt biscuits, three tiny holes marking each one?

Poor Smiley. She'd have become the broker of Jochim's rage for those first twenty-four hours when he might break the cardinal rule of no harm to the children.

Before she she left, Josanna had spent countless hours thinking through every scenario. All futile. The day she renounced her home, she refused to think about what the children would do, what they would think. Even now, a year later, her only memory of that day: turning off the electric kettle, a second later switching it back on, and worrying that the apartment could burn down. She'd almost unpacked her small bag, taken off the jeans she'd never worn before, and let her hair out from under the woolen hat. She'd stayed in the kitchen, picking at the snacks, crumbs littering the counters and her leather jacket, unable to move. Finally, she remembered D's face a few nights before, pinched in the glow of his night lamp, and her passing by, caressing his hair, him flinching, unconsciously, and in that moment, seeing him outgrown her.

***

One afternoon, walking with Lena past the salumeria, Josanna, unable to stop herself, had mumbled, "At least some mortadella." It was five pm. She'd been hungry since the watery soup that passed for lunch. Lena stopped in the street and raised a finger at Josanna, "Little choices add up to big ones." Josanna's eyes had widened but when she saw that Lena was serious, she said nothing. They kept walking. In the nine months since they'd enrolled in the weight-loss Lena had lost twenty-two kilos, Josanna seventeen. Together, they counted calories, and sweated at the gym, and shared cold water late at night when hunger woke them.

They avoided talking about the past. Their social worker, Maia, did enough of that, parsing what had happened, what they'd done, what they hadn't. It was her phrase, "Little choices add up to big ones," that Lena was echoing.

Josanna found the talk about choices – big and little ones – unending, the preoccupation of every woman there. "Why?" she wondered. So that they could dissect the results? Determine where their choices placed them in the spectrum from victim to survivor? Or as one of the shelter's monthly guest speakers had said, "Thriver."

In the shelter, she was known as the woman who had left her children behind by choice. Her choices bewildered them, bewildered her. She didn't fool herself that the children would be unscathed. Yet, there were things about Jochim that made her certain he wouldn't willfully hurt the children. His habit of tearing up at touching scenes in movies, laughing or coughing or shouting at the screen to cover up his emotion. His love for surprises, the spontaneous burst into song accompanied by wild hip shakes and flowering hands in the middle of the street, charming strangers and her. His self-pity the nights he lay his head on her arm, sending flares of pain all the way to her fingertips.

Her decision to leave, twelve years in, had no triggering incident, no final straw, no match lit, no break point. One night, as they watched television, A on the couch, legs folded over the arm of the sofa, controlling the remote, D absently plucking at his lip, Josanna standing at the door, a dawning that had been tucked away unfolded: soon, this would end, it would never end. The children would grow up, leave, she'd age, he'd age, they might even leave England, return to India, and they'd be the same story.

What story?

Once, a woman, waiting for a bus, was dazzled by how effortlessly a man asked her for directions. They boarded the bus, and he followed her home. Day after day, he stood at the bus stop, carrying an umbrella for her when it rained.

Once, the woman's hair loosened from the bun she wore. She shook it out in the street and twisted it back into a roll, the lift of her arms causing her breasts to rise. She did it to provoke him, he said, to entice other men. She started to wear her hair in braids.

Once, the woman asked the man to leave her alone. He said no, for ten days, a thousand times no, while her alarm swelled like a water balloon. On day eleven, he was waiting at the bus stop, doused in kerosene, ready to light a match. If she wanted him gone, he'd be out of her life forever, he said.

Once, the woman asked the man if he loved her. Too much, he said, didn't he prove his love daily?

***

The mouse was no longer on the desk, no longer anywhere in sight, but Josanna's hand trembled against her thigh. The invader! Determined to disrupt her one meal alone, away from Lena's friendship, the women at the shelter, Guilia's kindness.

Josanna contemplated the food in the carrier: the beef coagulating, the parathas half-wrapped in their foil winking in the sun. How much time had passed? Her stomach roiled at the thought of Giulia walking in on her. But the door to her little room was locked; even if she somehow missed the clang of the lift, she'd hear Giulia's steps tapping down the far end of the corridor.

She smoothed the foil and the crackle was loud, far louder than a square of aluminum could make. Could there be more than one critter? She spun the chair around, scraping the floor. "Jesus, please, no." Somehow the idea of one mouse was tolerable. Barely. But more than one multiplied instantly into an army.

She scanned the room again: vitrine clear, shelves intact, bookcases empty of anything but books. She opened the lid of the printer, a tabletop unlike the consumer models that occupied the middle of the main office. Blank white sheets glared up at her through the gaps in the cartridges and the paper roller. A rumble ran through Josanna, the floor. The entire building vibrated. Josanna gripped the printer. The mouse darted across the room. The rumbling stopped.

***

She and Lena were on the treadmill when Maia came in with the news. She was already sweating in the eight minutes since Lena had increased the incline on the walk-belt, and her mouth was so dry she couldn't feel her tongue.

Maia waved a piece of paper, her mouth wide and excited. Josanna switched off the treadmill and almost fell forward, grasping the arms of the machine to steady herself.

She panted, "Ennuh?" reverting to the Malayalam sound that replaced the question.

"He has agreeduh!" Maia handed Josanna the paper. "You are freeuh. Josy."

Lena hugged her. Josanna read the notice. Legal jargon, but the meaning was clear. She had been granted the divorce. But, "The children. It says, the children, they remain---" Her voice broke.

Maia bobbed her head. "Si, si. I have told you…"

Lena dragged Josanna to the seats. The three of them sat heavily, the chairs protesting. Josanna turned the paper over and over. When she sought divorce she'd petitioned for custody of the children. Maia, and the lawyer, a nice man called Guillermo, had warned her that she could lose. L'Aquila, so appealing on the television, and an actual refuge, had been an abysmal choice. Leaving her barely ten and eleven-year old sons was one thing, but crossing the border from England into Italy, had given Jochim the ammunition to label her departure as willful desertion. Guillermo shook his craggy head, "It's very hard to fight to bring them to you when you came so far away." And she had no evidence to submit in her defense, no bruises, no scars, none of the signs of trauma that someone like Lena had.

Somehow, she'd fed herself hope. It was what had kept her returning to the gym every day after she staggered out and swore to Lena that she was done with it all. It was what had replaced every pat of butter, every second helping. Now, Maia was picking the paper off the floor, where, somehow, it had dropped.

One morning, days later, Josanna awoke, her mouth wet with longing for her pepper-fried beef.

***

The sun shifted. Josanna breathed in, out. A breeze from the window lifted her hair. She wiped her brow, patted the sweat off her upper lip. She heaped bitter gourd and two scoops of the pepper beef on to her plate. The desk suddenly reverberated under her fingers. From somewhere far away, she heard a crash, or thunder, or a building's collapse. She closed her eyes. The roar stopped. She opened her eyes. The mouse sat on the windowsill. It was a baby, the color and size of a dust ball. Its ears were pink and its nose was a flesh-colored crayon tip. Josanna stared.

"What a fool you are, Josanna," she thought.

From the piazza she heard shouts, and somewhere in the distance, another boom. The mouse stopped sunning itself. The building quaked. The mouse's tiny head danced in the light, and Joanna considered how it would feel to stretch her hand out, and between her forefinger and thumb crush the mouse's skull. She wondered if she could do it, if she had it within her to flatten its body against the glass. Her food cooled against her wrist.

BIX GABRIEL is a writer, teacher at Butler University, fiction editor at *The Offing* magazine, and co-founder of TakeTwo Services. She has a M.F.A in Fiction from Indiana University, and is completing a novel involving the war on terror and Bangladesh's 1971 war for independence, set in New York City, Dhaka, and Guantánamo Bay.

www.ingramcontent.com/pod-product-compliance
Lightning Source LLC
Chambersburg PA
CBHW062027290426
44108CB00025B/2816